INDIA'S QUEST FOR SUSTAINABLE FARMING AND HEALTHY FOOD

INDIA'S QUEST FOR SUSTAINABLE FARMING AND HEALTHY FOOD

BY
BHARAT DOGRA AND
KUMAR GAUTAM

Vitasta

In the memory of Shri Ganesh Shankar Vidyarthi—Freedom Fighter and Eminent Editor who sacrificed his life for protecting human life and the unity of people of India

Published by
Renu Kaul Verma
Vitasta Publishing Pvt Ltd
2/15, Ansari Road, Daryaganj
New Delhi-110 002
info@vitastapublishing.com

ISBN 978-93-90961-61-0

First Edition 2022

MRP ₹495

Edited by MR Narayan Swamy
Cover and Layout by Somesh Kumar Mishra
Printed by Chaman Enterprises, New Delhi

CONTENTS

INTRODUCTION

In recent times, there has been an intense debate on agriculture and food policy in India and several other countries. This is not surprising as there are increasing concerns about the widespread distress faced by a large number of small and medium farmers as well as landless farm workers. The pressing need is for policy intervention to protect sustainable livelihoods.

In addition, in these times of climate change, there is growing concern to embrace the path of ecologically protective farming, thereby ensuring the availability of safe and healthy food.

It is very important to look at issues of farming and food from this perspective. I am very happy that at the right time Bharat Dogra and Kumar Gautam have come up with this book which looks at a wide range of issues. While there are so many books on farm and food policy, this one is written from the perspective of promoting sustainable livelihoods, protecting environment and ensuring the availability of safe and healthy food.

This book could not have come at a more appropriate time. The need for such a comprehensive work has been increasingly felt. As we search for policy options for promoting sustainable objectives, the ideas and the vision obtained here can be very useful.

Nearly two-thirds of the people in India live in rural areas. This is a critical reason why the world is deeply interested in how India resolves its rural livelihood issues. The farmers' movement in India has received support and sympathy from many parts of the world. Hence, the issues raised in this book are likely to be read with interest in India and abroad.

This book not only offers a well-reasoned critique of the approaches based on green revolution and GM crops but presents credible alternatives. This is a major strength of this book. Another welcome feature is that the authors show deep concern not just for land-owning farmers but for the landless rural households as well.

—Prof. Jagmohan Singh
Chairman, Shahid Bhagat Singh
Centenary Foundation and
Chairman All-India Forum for Right to Education

VOICES

The farmer differs from the industrialist in that the farmer is necessarily a nurturer, a preserver of the health of creatures.

The economy of industry is typically extractive. It takes, makes, uses and discards, it progresses, from exhaustion to pollution. Agriculture, on the other hand, rightly belongs to a replenishing economy, which takes, makes, uses and returns - it involves the return to the source, not just of fertility or of so-called wastes but also of care and affection.

The 'free market' - the unbridled play of economic forces – is bad for agriculture because it is unable to assign a value to things that are necessary to agriculture. It gives a value to agricultural products, but it cannot give a value to the sources of those products in the topsoil, the ecosystem, the farm, the farm family, or the farm community. Indeed, people who look at farming from the standpoint of the 'free market' do not understand the relation of product to source. They believe that the relation is merely mechanical because they believe that agriculture is or can be an industry. And the 'free market' is helpless to suggest otherwise.

—Wendell Berry
Farmer-philosopher, US

Policy Changes We Really Need

If the essence of the social-agro-ecology approach is to be captured in just one sentence, then it is a meeting point of two predominant concerns of providing secure, sustainable livelihoods of ordinary farmers and peasants on one hand and resolving major environmental, nutrition, health and safety issues on the other. In a nutshell, it is a meeting point of equality and environment protection, of justice and safety, of livelihoods and health. These main concerns are closely related to each other and should be pursued together.

—Bharat Dogra

1.1 Food, Farming Policy Needed

In recent years there has been a debate on agriculture and food in many parts of the world. More and more people realize that the existing farming and food system is progressing in the direction of corporatization. Also, the interests of small farmers and environment protection as well as production of safe and healthy food on a sustainable basis are being sacrificed and neglected. Hence, it is very important to carefully examine alternative policies to ensure secure livelihoods of small and medium farmers, production and availability of safe and healthy food, elimination of hunger and malnutrition, protection of environment and protection of all forms of life. It is necessary to explore and advance the huge potential of farming systems contributing to checking climate change while also adapting to more erratic and extreme weather.

Here we examine the most important aspects of a desirable food and farming system.

Safe, Nutritious, Adequate Food on Sustainable Basis

Policies should be directed towards cropping systems and rotations which give top priority to production of adequate, nutritious and safe food for now and in the future. More specifically, we need adequate amounts of grains, millets, legumes, vegetables, nuts, fruits and fodder combined with moderate amounts of salt, spices, sugar, milk, milk products, edible oils, tea, coffee, eggs, chicken and fish. Red meat and beef should be reduced as much as possible.

The consumption and production of high sugar, high fat and high salt processed foods should be much less. Tobacco and intoxicants should be curtailed to an even greater extent. The aim should be to reduce the consumption of tobacco in all forms and all alcoholic drinks by 90 percent or more. All this has to be achieved by strong policy measures and even stronger campaigns within a strong democratic framework.

The highest priority should be accorded to ensuring safe drinking and cooking water to all while emphasizing water conservation and saving practices. In addition, ensuring safe and easy, healthy and environment-friendly cooking fuel should be emphasized.

All food should be safe. This should be ensured by production and processing methods, legal provisions and educational campaigns. In particular, food should not be affected and contaminated by dangerous agri-chemicals. Food should not come from Genetically Modified (GM) crops. All GM crops should be banned.

Some of the restrictive policies suggested are in keeping with the needs of health and environment protection globally as well as requirements of animal welfare. These recommendations may differ for certain climate and geographical zones.

The first priority in farmland use is for producing safe, healthy and nutritious food. The next priority is for growing essential raw materials like cotton. Any other priority can be considered only after these two needs have been met.

A public distribution system to provide healthy food at subsidized price to all those in need as well as nutrition schemes play an important role in reducing hunger and malnutrition.

Sustainable Livelihood for Small Farmers, Farm Workers

Small and middle-level farmers should be respected as providers of safe and nutritious food. The prevailing attitude in many countries that their number should be necessarily reduced over time should be given up. Their livelihood based on production of safe and nutritious food should be strengthened. All the world's farmland should belong to small and middle-level farmers or their cooperatives. Land in excess of what can reasonably be cultivated by small and middle-level farmer households should be distributed among landless farm workers and rural people willing to practice sustainable farming.

Till this happens, other steps to improve their livelihood and welfare should be taken by the governments and communities. A fair wage should be ensured to farm workers. Landless persons who provide support to sustainable farming in artisan and ancillary activities should also get respect. Their welfare and sustainable livelihoods should be ensured.

All those who produce safe food using sustainable methods should be assured of a satisfactory selling price and marketing opportunities, including government procurement as well as direct sales to consumers. This should be strongly backed by public policy and community action. Small and medium traders who play non-exploitative and helpful roles and extend useful services based on experience should be accepted as integral parts of the marketing system. Exploitative and speculative traders and hoarders should be checked.

Rural livelihood opportunities in healthy and nutritious food processing should exist in villages. This can be supported initially by public funds. Suitable small-scale technology for this should be encouraged. Self-help groups and cooperatives can take up this work.

Rural livelihood opportunities in diverse areas which do not harm local environment should be promoted so that farmer households have access to additional ways to earn in or near their villages. In particular livelihoods in decentralized renewable energy, water conservation, afforestation, cottage-scale industry and Information Technology can be given a push. But such efforts should be supportive of prioritizing the production of safe and nutritious food. Farm livelihoods should be made sustainable for future generations by protecting the basic natural resource base (in the form of soil, soil organisms, water, greenery, supporting other forms of life and traditional knowledge of farming, seeds and related issues).

Land Fertility and Safe Food

Land has been degraded very badly and natural fertility has been eroded over vast areas due to several factors. These include harmful farming practices and inputs, deforestation, soil erosion, waterlogging, salinization and spread of deserts. Fertile land has been lost to rivers, brick kilns, mines and quarries as well as to industrial and urban use on a massive scale. Fertile land should be protected as much as possible.

Farm practices which are able to protect and/or restore natural fertility and organic matter should be followed. Maintaining and improving organic content of soil, based on local on-site decomposition of biological material, is crucial. Steps should be taken to prevent water logging and salinity and to reclaim land for farming if possible. Use of chemical fertilizers and harmful agri-chemicals should be minimized or avoided.

Mixed farming and crop rotations to sustain farm fertility should be encouraged. Growing trees and indigenous species can be taken up in a big way on land not suitable for agricultural crops as well as on degraded forest land. This will ensure sustainable livelihoods for landless people.

Conserve Water, Ensure Clean Drinking Water

High priority should be given to protect this most essential resource base of farmers and villagers. Rain harvesting and water conservation with community effort should get preference to maintain a proper water table. Highly water-intensive cropping systems or diversion for industrial or other uses beyond the carrying capacity of a region should be checked by public policy and community action. Maximum attention should be given for ensuring clean drinking and cooking water to all. The next priority should be to meet demand for hygiene needs and drinking water for all animals. Attention should be given to meeting the needs of sustainable farming. All wasteful and non-essential excessive uses of water should be discouraged.

Traditional Seeds and Biodiversity

A great diversity of seeds of food crops and trees as well as other useful crops have flourished on earth, nurtured by generations of farmers. Much of this has been lost in more recent times which emphasized monocultures of a very narrow genetic base. The rich diversity of traditional seeds should be saved and grown on ordinary farms. These should be widely encouraged among farmers. After a few years of such efforts, most farmers will not have to buy seeds from the commercial market. Free food received from nature, particularly natural forests, should be highly valued. The knowledge of local communities regarding this food should be respected and saved.

Low-Cost, Low External Input

Farm technology should avoid or minimize external inputs such as chemical fertilizers, pesticides and weedicides. There should be efforts based in local innovations to reduce use of expensive machinery and diesel to the extent possible. For example, a farmer's innovation in India, Mangal Turbine, can greatly help to reduce diesel use. Farm animals can contribute to reduce costs and external inputs. Dependence on commercial market for seeds can be minimized. The attempt should be to continue efforts to reduce costs and increase self-reliance as well as protect the environment.

Checking Greenhouse Gas Emissions

Increasing organic content of soil helps in absorption of carbon dioxide. Increasing green cover, protecting forests and creating new forests of indigenous species which seek to imitate natural forests will help in absorbing greenhouse gas emissions. Reducing chemical fertilizers and pesticides helps in reducing emissions of carbon dioxide and nitrous oxide. Diesel and machinery use should be reduced wherever possible. Long-distance marketing and wasteful packaging should be discouraged.

Adapting to Climate Change

Self-reliant farming systems which are also low-cost and low on external use systems will find it easier to adapt to climate change. Learning from traditional knowledge, protecting traditional seeds and bio-diversity will further improve this ability.

Ban GM Crops

All genetically modified crops (or so-called variations in the form of gene-edited crops) should be banned as these are harmful for human and animal health and can be very disruptive ecologically.

Protecting Friends of Farmers

Special efforts should be made to protect pollinators as well as all birds and insects which help farmers in various ways. Farm animals should be protected. Bullocks can still play an important role in ploughing and other farm activities. Mechanization is not inevitable and should be adopted only when it appears essential, and that too in a restrictive and careful way. Dairy and poultry activities should be taken up in an integrated manner with farming whenever possible. Adequate care must be given to the welfare of animals and birds. Earthworms should be protected, along with other soil-organisms which enrich soil.

Live With Nature's Ways

Perhaps the best way to promote sustainable farming and growth of safe food is to observe carefully the ways of nature and carry out farming in tune with it. Exactly the opposite of this happened while promoting industrial-style agriculture. This is how most of the damage to health and environment (as well as to sustainability of farms) was inflicted. We need to get the basics right.

No Single Formula or Person to Follow

Millions of farmers across the world have contributed and are contributing to sustainable production of safe and nutritious food. Several scientists have also done their bit. There is no single formula or single leader. The effort should be to learn from and build on the contribution made by farmers and some scientists. Region-specific solutions are necessary. So, a highly decentralized approach will be needed.

Decentralized Approach

A decentralized and participative attitude involving close cooperation of rural communities is vital. Farm scientists can certainly help but they should also be willing to learn from farmers. Above all, they should accept the basic perspective of sustainable and self-reliant farming for safe food in which external inputs are extremely low. Farmers' visits to areas of promising work, grassroot seminars, workshops, fairs and get-togethers should be encouraged.

Less Food Miles

Local markets should be linked with farmers while avoiding long-distance marketing except in case of special needs. Decentralized procurement by the government to secure a part of food crops to support public distribution system and nutrition schemes within a village should be boosted.

Public policy should encourage close links between farmers and neighboring urban consumers. The government should pay a fair price to purchase safe and nutritious food from farmers to supply to the public distribution system and nutrition programmes.

Nutrition Schemes, Kitchen Gardens

Nutrition schemes to end hunger and malnutrition should get adequate support. Kitchen gardens, particularly among the poorest sections who suffer more from hunger, must be promoted.

Check International Trade Which Exploits

Trade and other agreements detrimental to sustainable production of safe foods and livelihoods based on this should not be pursued. If they already exist, these should be cancelled. Agreements under which land and water sources necessary for sustaining rural communities are grabbed should be cancelled.

1.2 Agro-Ecology Is Key To Real Progress

Despite some local differences, the food and farming

systems of most countries have suffered from somewhat similar serious problems in recent decades.

Firstly, the problems of ordinary farmers have intensified despite government claims of increasing farm support. In many cases, this is related to heavy escalation of costs, in turn leading to debts. Many have lost the status of owner cultivators.

At the same time, power and control of big corporate interests have zoomed. There have also been complaints that the food produced by this system has problems related to safety, health and nutrition. It results in environmental ruin, biodiversity loss and excessive, avoidable GHG emissions. Analysts see all these problems to be related to each other.

The good news is that in thousands of places in various countries, efforts are being made by farmers and activists, in some cases helped by scientists and officials, to find solutions and alternatives which can avoid all or most problems while providing good yields or improving them further. A more organized thinking is emerging which can be called the social agro-ecology approach. This, in the near future, can provide the key to avoid all the above mentioned problems of food and farming systems while also checking climate change.

If the essence of the social agro-ecology approach is to be captured in one sentence, then it is a meeting point of two predominant concerns of providing secure, sustainable livelihoods to ordinary farmers and peasants on the one hand and resolving major environmental, nutrition, health and safety issues on the other. In a nutshell, it is a meeting point of equality and environment protection, of justice and safety, of livelihoods and health. These main concerns are closely related to each other and should be pursued together.

An important aspect of this approach is to observe and understand natural processes and to try best to work in harmony with this understanding. Nature is bountiful in several ways. Without human beings taking pains, nature contributes to fertility of soil, greening of land and proliferation of bio-diversity besides providing many edibles. While cultivating certain crops of their choice, human beings make interventions in this system. But it is best to do so only after understanding nature's bounty as there is so much that nature can contribute without any human struggle.

Earthworms and many micro-organisms work ceaselessly to make soil fertile. Legume plants have the extraordinary ability to make available nitrogen to soil. Bees, butterflies, many insects and birds provide invaluable service as pollinators. Frogs and owls help to control certain pests.

There are several plants which support the growth of each other. Mixed farming of wheat with gram can help to maintain fertility of soil. The same is true of mixed cropping of other cereals and legumes. Similarly, if proper rotation is selected, this too helps to maintain soil fertility. Some tender plants grow better in the shade of some dense or taller plants. Some creepers need the support of strong stems of certain plants. Generally time-honored mixed farming practices and rotations are very admirably linked to nutrition needs of people as well as soil. They are also in conformity with local rainfall and water access.

A lot can be gained in terms of improving yields while at the same time maintaining soil fertility if this aspect of which crop grows well with another crop is understood and if crop rotation is appreciated. I have met women farmers growing over two dozen crops on a small one- or two-acre farm and sustaining good yields, mainly on the basis of this understanding.

Similarly, the relationships between farm animals and birds (and in some cases fish also) on the one hand and crops and trees on the other hand needs to be understood. The diversity of seeds is important and the precise suitability of seeds of a particular variety for a particular type of land should be well understood. Other aspects of seed varieties should also be known in order to realize their proper potential. Hence, it is important to give importance to collection and maintenance of traditional seed varieties and to promote their mutual exchange among farmers so that more of this traditional, rich bio-diversity can flower in fields.

Farming based on such care and understanding is only possible on the basis of hard working small (and medium) farmers. The other part of social agro-ecology is to ensure that the small farmers remain the base of agriculture and farmland does not pass into the hands of big landlords and corporates. If some land or much of land has passed into their hands, it should be taken back and redistributed among landless or near landless rural households.

Social agro-ecology is essentially a system of small

farmers who are encouraged towards increasing levels of cooperation and mutual help to better understand nature and natural processes.

Women farmers make an important contribution in most small farmer systems and are known for hard work and creativity. Hence more encouragement and recognition should be extended to women farmers in social agro-ecology.

Agro-ecology has the potential to provide highly creative, satisfying, sustainable livelihoods to a very large number of people while protecting nature and ensuring adequate healthy, nutritious and safe food. It is admirably suited also for reduction of GHG emissions and their absorption. Hence, this is clearly the most desirable pattern for farm policy.

Getting Rid of Green Revolution Myths

I explain that I do not share the opinions which have been expressed as to Indian Agriculture being, as a whole, primitive and backward, but I believe that in many parts there is little or nothing that can be improved. Whilst where agriculture is manifestly inferior, it is more generally the result of the absence of facilities which exist in the better districts than from inherent bad systems of cultivation.... I may be bold to say that it is a much easier task to propose improvements in English agriculture than to make really valuable suggestions for that of India... the conviction has forced itself upon me that, taking everything together and more especially considering the conditions under which Indian crops are grown, they

> *are wonderfully good. At his best the Indian raiyat or cultivator is quite as good as, and in some respect the superior of, the British farmer, while at his worse it can only be said that this state is brought out largely by an absence of facilities for improvement which is probably unequalled in any other country... I have remarked in earlier chapters about the general excellence of the cultivations, the crops grown here are numerous and varied, much more indeed than in England.*
>
> —**John Augustus Voelcker**
> The Royal Agricultural Society of England
> (Invited by the British Government to suggest improvements in farming in India, 1893)

2.1 Green Revolution – Myth and Reality

One of the most enduring myths of the development experience of India has been that without the green revolution varieties, the country would have starved as enough food could not have been produced. Faced with mounting evidence of the adverse impacts of green revolution, its diehard supporters say, 'This price had to be paid as otherwise India could never have produced enough food for its people.'

In this chapter we try to counter the myth with ten arguments.

i Firstly, the yield in the pre-green revolution years was rising at a reasonably good pace. In the case of some important crops like rice, the increase was in fact higher than in the post green revolution years.

ii Secondly, eminent experts found that the farmers were making very good use of their resources and conditions and that their technologies were very sound and suitable.

iii Thirdly, we present evidence that many indigenous varieties have yields higher than green revolution varieties without using the heavy doses of agri-chemicals needed by the latter.

iv Fourthly, before green revolution seeds were introduced, far from facing emergency conditions, Indian scientists were on the verge of a major breakthrough for raising yields based on indigenous varieties, at least in the case of the most important food crop.

v Fifthly, land reforms too would have opened up the doors for pushing up productivity significantly but this path was neglected.

vi Sixthly, in many contexts green revolution seeds increased problems right from the early days and several warnings about this were given by senior scientists.

vii We outline the many problems the green revolution technology has created.

viii We look at persisting high levels of malnutrition and under-nutrition.

ix We argue that the green revolution technology should be given up now and alternatives explored.

x There is a need for more comprehensive research on this issue.

I

A comparison is made for agricultural yields for two periods – roughly the 15 pre-green revolution years with approximately the 15 post-green revolution years.

An overview of the farm productivity before and after the green revolution is provided in the 12th Plan document in two important tables. (See Tables 1 and 2). Clearly, despite the much higher use of chemical fertilisers and pesticides in the green revolution phase, the growth of farm yield on the whole was in fact lower.

Table 1 Average Annual Growth Rates in Yields per Hectare

Crop	Pre-Green Revolution 1951-52 to 1967-68	Green Revolution 1968-69 to 1980-81
Wheat	3.7	3.3
Rice	3.2	2.7
Jowar	3.4	2.9
Bajra	2.6	6.3
Maize	4.8	1.7
Coarse Cereals	2.6	1.5
Pulses	2.3	-0.2
Oilseeds	1.3	0.8
Cotton	3.0	2.6
Sugarcane	1.6	3.1

Table 2 Growth of Value of Output (2004-05 Prices) (Period averages of annual growth rates)

Crop	Pre-Green Revolution 1951-52 to 1967-68	Green Revolution 1968-69 to 1980-81
Cereals	4.2	3.4
Pulses	3.0	0.7
Oilseeds	3.2	1.8
Sugars	3.3	4.1
Fibres	4.4	2.5
Non-Horticulture crops	3.2	2.7
Horticulture	2.6	4.2

(Source: 12th Plan Document)

* Slight adjustments have been made in years keeping in view the way the data was available in different official publications. We show to what extent the green revolution or HYV (High Yielding Varieties) were spread in India during these years and the accompanying huge increase in chemical fertilisers, pesticides and other expenses.

The period after mid-60s is generally regarded as the green revolution phase of Indian agriculture. The most important feature of this technology boom was the introduction of HYV seeds. There can be several types of HYVs.

For example, in Madhya Pradesh, some indigenous rice varieties have been found to give very high yields even by traditional methods of cultivation without using chemical fertilisers. However, in the official programmes of improved agriculture in India, generally only those (dwarf, non-lodging) varieties which gave high yields when fed by chemical fertilisers, were included. Therefore, we should call them HRVs (High Response Varieties) rather than HYVs. However, for the sake of comparability with other publications, here also we use the improper word 'HYVs'.

The extent of the spread of the new varieties is made clear by Table 3:

Table 3

Area under HYV Programme (Million ha.)

Crop	Total Area under various crops	Area under HYV in 1978-79	Percentage	Target of area under HYV in 1984-85
Paddy	40.48	16.90	40	25.00
Wheat	22.64	16.10	75	19.00
Maize	05.76	02.10	40	02.00
Jowar	16.14	03.10	20	05.00
Bajra	11.39	02.90	25	05.00
Total	96.41	41.10	41	56.00

Note: This table has been derived from tables 1.6 and 1.10 of the Economic Survey 1980-81 and table 9.1 of the Sixth Five Year Plan Document. Jowar and bajra are coarse cereals.

Along with the spread of HYV seeds, as part of the 'package deal', the use of chemical fertilisers, chemical pesticides and agriculture machinery went up greatly. To spread and strengthen the new technology, investment in farm research besides education and extension increased.

From 1952-53 to 1965-66, about 5,228 thousand tonnes of fertilisers were used. During the 14-year period from 1966-67 to 1979-80, this zoomed to 35,487 thousand tonnes.

The use of chemical pesticides (technical grade) skyrocketed from negligible amounts to nearly 60,000 tonnes per annum in later years.

From 1950-51 to 1965-66, the area under irrigation increased by 11 million hectares; from 1965-66 to 1979-80, this doubled to 22 million hectares.

In 1966, India had 53,000 tractors. By 1978, this touched a whopping 367,000 tractors.

The number of oil engines rose from 470 thousand in 1966 to 1,754 thousand in 1974 and of electric pumps sets from 415 thousand in 1966 to 2,786 thousand in 1976.

From 1950-51 to 1965-66, a modest Rs 120 million was incurred on agricultural research. From 1966-67 to 1979-80, nearly Rs 4,400 million was spent.

Similarly, from 1950-51 to 1965-66, agriculture education cost was just Rs 2.5 million; from 1966-67 to 1977-78, this increased to Rs 670 million.

In view of the massive increase in the expenditure on farm inputs, research and education, farm yields should have increased at a much higher rate than in the previous 15 years. This was more so in view of the prevailing low yield of Indian agriculture when compared to world averages.

In reality, while the yields did rise in the case of some crops, it declined in others, and remained nearly steady in some. This is evident from the statistics given in the succeeding paragraphs.

Table 4

Yield of major Crops (kgs per hectare) in the pre-1966 period

S.No.	Period	Yield of Paddy	Yield of Wheat	Yield of Jowar	Yield of Bajra	Yield of Maize	Yield of Pulses	Yield of 5 Major Oilseeds
	(1)	(2)	(3)	(4)	(5)	(6)	(7)	(8)
1.	1950-51	668	655	353	288	547	441	481
2.	First five year Plan (1951-56)	817	738	436	309	750	474	465
3.	Second 5 year Plan (1956-61) Average	915	757	497	303	857	493	510
4.	Third 5 year Plan (1962-67) Average	986	834	486	342	1000	466	487
5.	Annual Plans (1966-69) Average	992	1062	527	363	1018	468	477
6.	Fourth 5 year Plan (1969-74) Average	1112	1272	488	475	1052	491	541
7.	Fifth 5 year Plan (1974-79) Average	1201	1437	669	462	1066	505	579
8.	1979-80	1082	1436	685	377	966	385	523

Table-4 is based on Annexure 9.2 of the Sixth Plan Document

In the case of paddy, the average yield of the First Plan years (1951-56) was 22 percent higher than in 1950-51. During the Second Plan (1956-61), the average yield rose by 12 percent and in the next plan (1961-66) by 8 percent. During the three annual plans (1966-69), the average yield went up by only 0.7 percent. The Fourth Plan (1969-74) saw an increase of 12 percent and the Fifth Plan (1974-79) 8 percent. Compared to the Fifth Plan average, in 1979-80 the yield decreased by 10 percent. Thus, on the whole, the rate of increase in paddy yield was higher during the first 15 years. And rice is by far the most important crop of India.

In respect of wheat, the rate of increase of the average yield during the first, second and third plans respectively was 13 percent, 3 percent and 10 percent. The post-1966 performance was better. The average yield increased by 27 percent during the annual plan period, by 20 percent during the Fourth Plan period and by 13 percent during the Fifth Plan period.

Jowar's performance was moderately better post 1966. During the First and Second plans, the average yield increased by 12 and 14 percent respectively and declined by 2 percent in the Third Plan period. The average yield rose during the annual plans by 7.5 percent and then decreased by nearly as much during the Fourth Plan. However, during the Fifth Plan, this went up significantly by nearly 39 percent.

Bajra: The First Plan saw the average yield go up by 7 percent. It declined by 2 percent in the Second Plan and again rose by 13 percent in the Third Plan. During the annual plans, this increased by 6 percent and by 30 percent during the Fourth Plan. This decreased by 2.5 percent in the Fifth Plan and then again by 18 percent in 1979-80 (compared to Fifth Plan average).

Maize: The performance was much better in the pre-1966 phase. In the First Plan period, the average yield rose by 37 percent, by 14 percent in the Second Plan and 16 percent in the Third Plan. This went up during the annual plans by only 1.8 percent, during the Fourth Plan by 3.4 percent and during the Fifth Plan by 1.3 percent. In 1979-80, the yield declined by nearly 10 percent.

Pulses: The average yield increased by 8 percent during the First Plan and declined by 4.5 percent and 7 percent in the next two plans. During the annual plans, the average yield remained the same. It increased moderately by 5 and 3 percent during the next two plans. However, in 1979-80, this fell very heavily by 24 percent.

In the case of five major oilseeds, the yield declined by 3 percent during the First Plan, increased by 10 percent in the Second Plan and declined by 4.5 percent in the Third Plan. During the annual plans, the yield declined further by 2 percent and rose during the next two plans by 11 percent and 7 percent respectively. In 1978-79, it fell by 10 percent.

Thus overall, there is little evidence of better performance in the post 1966 phase in the rate of increase of yield despite the massive increase in spending on irrigation, fertilisers, pesticides, agricultural machinery, research and education.

II

Even during British rule, several British and European experts spoke glowingly of the rich traditions and scientific basis of the cultivation practices pursued by Indian farmers.

In 1889, Dr John Augustus Voelcker of the Royal Agricultural Society of England, deputed by the British government to study Indian agriculture, toured the country extensively for over one year. His report, published in 1893, has often been cited as an authoritative work on Indian agriculture of this period.

The essence of what Dr Voelcker said can be summarized in the following extract:

I explain that I do not share the opinions which have

been expressed as to Indian Agriculture being, as a whole, primitive and backward, but I believe that in many parts there is little or nothing that can be improved. Whilst where agriculture is manifestly inferior, it is more generally the result of the absence of facilities which exist in the better districts than from inherent bad systems of cultivation.... I may be bold to say that it is a much easier task to propose improvements in English agriculture than to make really valuable suggestions for that of India... the conviction has forced itself upon me that, taking everything together and more especially considering the conditions under which Indian crops are grown, they are wonderfully good. At his best the Indian raiyat or cultivator is quite as good as, and in some respect the superior of, the British farmer, while at his worse it can only be said that this state is brought out largely by an absence of facilities for improvement which is probably unequalled in any other country... I have remarked in earlier chapters about the general excellence of the cultivations, the crops grown here are numerous and varied, much more indeed than in England. That the cultivation should often be magnificent is not to be wondered at when it is remembered that many of the crops have been known to the raiyats for several centuries, rice is a prominent instance in point.

More specially, he stated: To take the ordinary acts of husbandry, nowhere would one find better instances of keeping land scrupulously clean from weeds, of ingenuity in device of water-raising appliances, of knowledge of soils and their capabilities as well as of the exact time to sow and to reap, as one would in Indian agriculture, and this not at its best only but at its ordinary level. It is wonderful, too, how much is known of rotation, the system of mixed crops and fallowing. It is certain that I, at least, have never seen a more perfect picture of careful cultivation, combined with hard labour, perseverance and fertility of resource, than I have seen at many of the halting places in my tour. Such are the gardens of Mahi, the fields of Nadiad and many others.

An important asset of traditional Indian agriculture was the well-developed irrigation system. Irrigation by wells is at once the most widely distributed system, and also the one productive of the finest examples of careful cultivation..... Further as regards wells, one cannot help being struck by the skill with which a supply of water is first found by the native cultivators, then by the construction of the wells, the kinds of wells and their suitability to the surroundings and means of the people; also by the various devices for raising water each of which has a distinct reason for its adoption. All these are most interesting points with which I am not called upon to deal, for I see little to improve in them which the cultivator does not know perfectly well.

Another aspect, less widely realized, was a scientific rotation system. Voelcker pointed out that it is a mistake to suppose that rotation is not understood or appreciated in India. Frequently, more than one crop at a time may be seen occupying the same ground but one is apt to forget that this is really an instance of rotation being followed. It is not an infrequent practice, when drilling a cereal crop, such as jowar (sorghum) or some other millet, to put in at intervals a few drills of some leguminous crop such as arhar.

There are many systems in ordinary use which are far

more complicated than the above. For instance, not only may there be rows of crops, side by side, as noticed above, but the alternating rows may be made up of mixtures of different crops, some of them quick growing and requiring both sun and air, and thus being reaped after the former have been cleared off. Again, some are deep rooted plants while others are surface feeders. Some require the shelter of other plants and some thrive alone. The whole system appears to be one designed to cover the barrenness and consequent loss to the soil.

Voelcker was not the only agricultural scientist to point out these assets of traditional agriculture in India. There were other scientists, experts and scholars too.

J Millison, who later became the first Inspector General of Agriculture in India, published in 1901 the *Text Book of Indian Agriculture*. Like Voelcker, Millison stressed the positivity of the implements used traditionally in India.

I believe that the implements in ordinary use are entirely suitable for the conditions of Indian agriculture. This statement may be objected to by other authorities, but if such is the case, l am afraid, I cannot change a deliberately expressed opinion. To those who are skeptical, I can show in parts of the Presidency cultivation by means of indigenous tillage implement only, which in respect of neatness, thoroughness and profitableness cannot be excelled by the best gardeners or the best farmers in any part of the world. That statement I deliberately make and am quite prepared to substantiate.

AO Hume, in *Agricultural Reform in India* (1878), wrote about weed-control by Indian farmers. As for weeds, their wheat fields would, in this respect, shame ninety-nine out of hundred of those in Europe. You may stand in some high old barrow-like village site in Upper India, and look down on all sides one wide sea of waving wheat broken only by dark green islands of mango groves — many square miles of wheat and not a weed or blade of grass above six inches in height to be found amongst it.

Hume's tribute to the grain-storage practices of Indian farmers is no less glowing. 'They are great adepts in storing grain, and will turn grain out of rough earthen pits, after 20 years absolutely uninjured. They know the exact state of ripeness to which grain should be allowed to stand in different seasons.'

Another expert, Sir George Watt, observed in 1891: It must in fact be admitted that we have to fall back on Dr Buchnan Hamilton's idea that the chief differences between the thousands of farms of cultivated rice varieties hinge on their properties and peculiarities under cultivation. These peculiarities the Indian cultivator, through the time -honoured practices of his ancestors, is able to recognize far more accurately than botanical science has as yet been able to explain. He determines the suitability or otherwise of this form and that to its contemplated environment with a degree of confidence quite inexplicable.

Dr RH Richharia, a former Director of the Central Rice Research Institute, did extensive and invaluable work in cooperation with farmers, particularly in Madhya Pradesh, Chhattisgarh and Odisha. He wrote: Invariably I found in rice areas some rice growers taking keen interest in their local rice varieties and as they are very much absorbed in them they have all praise for them, so much so that they trace back the history of individual rice varieties to their ancestry with their utility. I also observed that some of them would identify their rice varieties in their own way (not in terms of the modern knowledge of Botany) which amounted to thousands. This inherent and intuitional faculty of farmers in selection and maintenance of thousands of rice cultivars, gradually being accumulated and descended down for unknown centuries, ever since rice first originated, must be preserved and exploited for the advantage of the present generation and to ensure the safety of those still unborn.

It may be questioned. Will the rice cultivators absorb and follow up these methods? The answer is that during our extensive surveys of the rice regions of India, we observed that the rice farmers have been following more complicated systems to keep their rice culture vigorous and maintaining their thousands of rice varieties from times immemorial.

III

In Madhya Pradesh (which then included Chhattisgarh), Dr Richharia's research revealed that several indigenous rice varieties gave high yields without the use of chemical fertilizers and pesticides.

Unfortunately, these traditional high-yielding varieties were not given official recognition. As Dr Richharia noted: In fact in every rice growing locality, the growers themselves tell us which of their own varieties are high yielding to which they stick. But under the extension services, the definition of high yielding rice variety is different which necessarily involves a dwarfing gene and, therefore, growers' own high yielding varieties are not recognised which are estimated to be 8 or 9 percent in MP.

Writing about rice, India's most important food crop, Dr Richharia said the importance of traditional wisdom of farmers is tied up with the fact that different varieties are needed for varying conditions. If we were to think of a single characteristic feature of the rice crop which yields food for millions, it cannot be anything else unless it be its (1) variability in the form of thousands of its cultivars, spread in India and in other rice growing belts of the world. This is because of the rice plant's flexible genetic make-up and mutational power to adaption. This means the concept of 'wider adaptability' does not work in rice and (2) the rice farmers stick to their own varieties as they possess their deep knowledge to harvest a crop even under the most stress situations and they also possess high yielding varieties of their own which are generally not included in extension programmes.

In a survey carried out in Madhya Pradesh in 1971-74,8 percent of the indigenous rice types were observed to fall under the category of high yielding types, fixing the minimum limit of 3,705 kg/Ha.

An important publication, written by Dr Richharia in 1977 from which we will quote extensively, was titled *A strategy for Rice Production to Ensure Sustained Growth in Madhya Pradesh*.

The first and foremost fact this publication emphasised is the ready availability of several indigenous high yielding varieties with yields (obtained at much less expense) comparable to or greater than the exotic high yielding varieties. In view of this finding's significance, which is still not widely known, we quote from this document in detail.

During 1975, nucleus seeds of 967 improved cultures under BD (Baronda) series were sent out to different locations (Government seed multiplication farms and farmers' holdings) in 17 districts, mostly tested under normal fertility with no plant protection measures applied. The result, obtained from eleven districts, are presented in Appendices 1 to 5 of ARRC Note No 9. The average of 121 entries works out to be 3,984 kg/Ha of paddy grain or 2,669 kg/Ha of rice. In terms of the definition of a high yielding variety in respect of yield 3,705 kg/Ha, as accepted by the MP Agriculture Department, the improved material recommended here can be accepted as high yielding.

Comparative high yields observed in some trials are detailed in this publication.

'There are many good cultures tested at Seoni Malwa during 1978 which can be quoted to establish that productive germ-plasm exists in different parts of Madhya Pradesh which can be utilized in increasing rice yields.'

This document offers direct proof to establish that the selected material in the form of BD series possesses superior yield potential which can from the basis to increase rice production in immediate future with added advantage that they are palatable and they show resistance to pest and to periodical drought to some extent.

'They have been bred under no plant protection umbrella. This production potential must be tapped and antagonism against indigenous types has to disappear.'

The document separately describes the already

identified indigenous high yielding, early-maturing, drought-resistant, scented and special flavour varieties.

'The surveys carried out so far have disclosed the existence of over 237 scented varieties, maintained by the growers in the state. Such scented varieties are Chinnor of Balaghat (village Kaidi), Dubraj of Sehawa Nagri and Kali Muchh of Dabra (Gwalior).'

Very long grain varieties such as Dokra Dekri and Raja Bangla were found especially useful for preparing murra. Dokra Dekri is the world's longest recorded rice. Chilko variety of rice was found to be used by advasis (tribals) for making good chapatis. Khowa variety of rice had the taste of dried milk.

Another document, prepared by Dr Richharia and his staff at the Adaptive Rice Research Center near Baronda in Raipur, was drafted in 1974 (*Adaptive Rice Research Note No 5 – Our Strategy on the Rice Production Front*) and makes important observations. One relates to experiments which show indigenous varieties can perform better then exotic HYVs such as Ratna and Sona.

In an experiment carried out at the center (Baronda), evidence was available to conclude that under identical conditions, the two indigenous varieties, Surmatia and Baikoni, at 40 kg N/Ha with cultural manipulations (Phaltai system) outperformed or remained at par with HYVs Ratna and Sona (fertilized at 100 kg/N/Ha) under Biyasi system with no plant protection adopted.

This indicates a value of far reaching significance and has a relevance to the existing situation when Biyasi is practised in 92 percent of the area in Chhattisgarh, and fertilizers and plant protection chemicals are in short supply. This indicates that the dwarfs are not suited to the Biyasi system and that they stand to lose considerably in the absence of plant protection measures with lower doses of fertilizers and without plant protection measures the adapted indigenous varieties yield better or remain at par with the dwarfs, grown with high doses of fertilizers For the dwarfs the two inputs are most essential viz fertilizers and plant protection chemicals. In the absence of any one, they suffer heavily and therefore the selected tall varieties are to be preferred.

Dr Richharia emphasised that wisdom of local farmers regarding diverse rice varieties should be utilised as the major resource for improving rice cultivation. He emphasised that rice farmers who possess intimate knowledge of their rice varieties should be involved in the research effort.

'A special advantage associated with indigenous high yielding rice germplasm identified for different tracts and situations is that it possesses a good level of resistance to environmental stress and common diseases and pests, coupled with local preference for palatability.'

Dr Richharia wrote: It may be of interest to record that during our survey in the Chhattisgarh area we came across rice growers in a remote area, maintaining a large collection of rice varieties, year after year, associated with local customs. This also explains how thousands of varieties are being descended down for centuries. Naturally such collections served as 'Local treasuries', but in the absence of an organisation to encourage such private endeavours, the valuable rices are fast disappearing, due to deliberate attempts.

IV

By the mid-60s, the Central Rice Research Institute (CRRI) had emerged as the most important centre of rice research in India, and one of the most important in the world. It was around this period that research relating to an important technology – clonal propagation of rice – was reaching a decisive stage under the guidance of the CRRI Director Dr Richharia. The technology being tried held the exciting potential of significantly increasing rice yield based on indigenous rice varieties and rapidly spreading the improved varieties over a very wide area.

Nearly two decades later, Dr Richharia recollected the goings-on around him at a seminar on the 'Crisis of Modern Science' held in Malaysia in November 1986 in the following words:

'The possibility of exploitation of hybrid vigour by the application of clonal propagation in rice in later generations was demonstrated at CRRI and the results were published in a British Journal *Nature* in 1962 entitled *Clonal Propagation as a Practical Means of Exploiting Hybrid Vigour in Rice*. The technique was also explained by me at a seminar held at IRRI in 1963. We were systematically proceeding with the work at eleven centres in India with success. We had just reached the stage to revolutionise rice production, but all the centres were closed down and instead HYV programme of IRRI with dwarfing genes was launched suppressing the CRRI work.

'At the later part (of my stay in CRRI) I passed my time in great distress because I opposed the interference imposed by IRRI (International Rice Research Institute) authorities who received at the initial stage all technical help from me and my staff, including the rice germ plasm and even building plans to build up that Institute at Los Banos in the Philippines. IRRI were to impose on CRRI their programme and take away its initiative and supremacy which I resisted to protect our interest. The IRRI programme dealt exclusively with the rice culture with dwarfing genes and replace the indigenous rice varieties by IRRI bred IR HYV series and under the pretext of exchange programme to collect the entire rice germ plasm directly and indirectly through trainees, visitors, some with our knowledge and some without our knowledge, sometimes even bringing their rice cultures personally to India without quarantine certificates.

My devoted band of young scientists soon alerted me and I realized that our programme and findings on rice production technology which had reached a stage to introduce revolution in upgrading India's rice productivity were being suppressed, useful projects being withdrawn and being superseded in preference to IRRI's programme. I, as head of CRRI, had no other option but to oppose this interference openly in the interest of my country on the food front.'

It is clear from this testimony that much better alternatives compared to green revolution were available and had reached an advanced stage to increase production in a sustainable way but these were not allowed to progress and were even sabotaged.

V

Many studies indicated that properly implemented land reforms would have helped to significantly raise yields but this path was ignored.

Land reforms are helpful for protecting land fertility, sustainable use of land as well as wastelands' development as hard working peasants are likely to work more sincerely for soil and water conservation and related works.

For somewhat similar reasons, land reforms can also lead to a rise in farm productivity, that too on the farms of the poor. This view is supported by several international studies.

In a widely quoted publication, *Agriculture Towards 2000*, the Food & Agriculture Organization (FAO) emphasized that more equal land distribution is likely to increase productivity of land. 'It is important to stress here that yields per hectare are as high on small as on large farms or, under traditional agriculture, even higher. With a few notable exceptions, total output per hectare is higher on small farms, chiefly because their intensity of land use is higher.'

This view of FAO is supported by a six-country study by the International Labour Organization (ILO) which estimated that 'if land were equally distributed among all agricultural families (including the landless), and the new equal holdings achieved yields equal to present holdings of the same size and used a similar level of inputs, food output could potentially rise by anything from 10 percent (Pakistan) and 28 percent (Colombia and a rice-growing Malaysian region) to 80 percent in northeastern Brazil. Such a radical redistribution is, of course, rarely attempted but the figures indicate the theoretical potential.'

VI

On March 15, 1966, the Director of CRRI wrote a confidential and important letter to the Director General, Indian Council of Agricultural Research, Delhi: The International Rice Research Institute (IRRI), Manila, has been sending a lot of rice experimental material from time to time into this country, and these are grown in several states. It has come to my notice that most of this material is susceptible to a very peculiar disease, not known to this country so far; it is suspected to be a virus.

Having sounded this warning, the Director stated: I may point out that in the last Rice Research Workers' Conference during November 1965, IR 9-60 has been recommended as one of the donor parents for hybridization programme in the various rice-growing states. But this material, as has already been reported earlier, has been observed by me at CRRI and two other centres to be infected with the yellowing disease at an early vegetative phase. I may also inform that from some source I have learnt that IR 9-60 is not only susceptible to Tungru virus, but also to bacterial blight. As such it is not a desirable material for being used as a donor parent; if used, it may spread diseases whereever the material is grown. Under these circumstances it would soon be beyond our control.

That some sort of inoculum of this dreadful disease is getting built up in the country is evident from the fact that Taichung Native I which was not showing the yellowing of leaves in the early vegetative phase of the summer crop of last year has now exhibited it. Since the Ministry of

Food and Agriculture has a huge programme of speedily spreading this variety in the near future, timely action has to be taken against any future catastrophe of the kind being observed now.

Having sounded these warnings, the Director of CRRI made the following recommendations:

a) Wherever rice cultures from IRRI are being grown should be carefully watched for which instructions have to be issued.
b) Action will have to be taken to withdraw the hybridization programme recommended under item A (2) of the Rice Research Workers Conference involving IR 9-60 as the donor parent.
c) Restrictions will have to be imposed against the free import of IRRI rice material by any source other than CRRI.

Unfortunately, these warnings and recommendations were ignored by the top authorities. Instead, the Director was pre-maturely retired. The pest and disease susceptible varieties were allowed to spread.

All this proved very harmful for India's agriculture. The results became evident all too soon. The massive damage became so worrying that a special task force of eminent experts was constituted in 1979 to examine the problem of rice breeding. Dr Richharia was called back from his retirement to head this task force as his advice was considered invaluable.

This task force report stated firmly: Most of the HYVs are derivatives of T(N) 1 or IR 8 and, therefore, have the dwarfing gene of dee-geo-woo-gen. This narrow genetic base has created alarming uniformity, causing vulnerability to diseases and pests. Most of the released varieties are not suitable for typical uplands and low lands which together constitute about 75 percent of the total rice area of the country. To meet these situations, we need to reorient our research programmes and strategies.

Referring to the problem of narrow genetic base at another place, the task force said, 'A cursory look at the pedigree of the different rice varieties released in India reveals that a very narrow germ plasm base is involved. It is also noticed that many times the same female parent is involved in the cross combination.'

Thus, though the earlier warnings of Dr Richharia were now confirmed by the actual experience of about 13 years and supported by the country's eminent rice-breeders represented in the task force, these warnings too were ignored to a large extent. The official rice programme/policy centred on exotic dwarf HYVs with a narrow genetic base continued as before.

VII

We present some of adverse impacts of green revolution on the existing food, agriculture and nutrition situation in India:

- Persistence of very high levels of malnutrition and under-nutrition, a problem which has many aspects.
- High rates of depletion of natural fertility of farmland, including alarming loss of several micro-nutrients.

- High fall in water table in vast areas.
- Many cases of poisoning of people by pesticides and other agri-chemicals, loss of other forms of life and spread of serious diseases.
- Botanic holocaust in the form of loss of thousands of crop varieties and threats to others.
- Loss of invaluable traditional wisdom relating to agriculture and seeds and breakdown of system of passing knowledge from one generation to another.
- Heavy burden of food, fertiliser and agriculture subsidies often as a result of the intolerably high costs of transporting food across vast areas.
- Much diminished per capita availability of pulses and legumes.
- Loss of taste and nutrition in food crops.
- Reduced availability of fodder.
- Serious hazards and pollution in more intensive green revolution areas.
- High drain on foreign exchange as India emerged as the highest importer of chemical fertilisers. Most feedstocks of domestic production of fertilisers are also imported. High imports of ediable oil and pulses are also a drain.

VIII

The per capita net availability of cereals and pulses declined from 468.7 grams per day in 1961 to 437.1 grams in 2010. The per capita net availability of pulses fell from 61.0 grams in 1961 to 35.4 grams in 2010.

The following statistics reveal the extent to which high levels of malnutrition exist in India. This data is for the time period of around four decades after the introduction of green revolution.

- In rural India, the body mass index (BMI) of 35 percent of people is below the norm of 18.5 (values below 18.5 indicate chronic energy deficit). If only Scheduled Castes are considered, then 38 percent have BMI below 18.5. In the case of Scheduled Tribes, as many as 42 percent have BMI below 18.5.
- The National Nutrition Monitoring Bureau (NNMB) surveys also show significant anaemia in 55 percent of men and 70 percent of women as well as deficiency of other main nutrients including Vitamins and minerals.
- Child malnutrition rate was estimated at around 44 percent in an assessment by the Nandi Foundation, an estimate not much different from earlier estimates of NNMB.
- According to the National Family Health Survey-III (2005-06), almost half of all the under-5 deaths were closely associated with poor nutritional status.

Large scale deforestation in India has had many adverse consequences. A relatively neglected one has been the diminishing availability of edible fruits, flowers, roots, tubers and seeds for tribals and other villagers living near forests – highly nutritious food which was available free to them in plenty in the not-too-distant past. The increasing commercialization of forestry and forestry practices has also led to the diminishing availability of free food from forests. Traditional tree species rich in food resources are being replaced by commercial tree species useful mainly for industries.

A document prepared by the Tribal and Harijan Welfare Department described how natural forests, particularly the Sal forests of Bastar, are like a repository of all sorts of edible fruits, roots and shoots. Their availability is the maximum during the 'lean' period of the year (March/April to August/September) when the people's need for a substitute or an alternative to their cereal diet is the most. These produce also act as a nutrient additive. A list of 22 types of fruits, 8 flowers, 14 leaves, 29 roots and 11 seeds used as food is given in this report.

Apart from these, three are several other food related benefits from forests such as the collection of fuel and fodder, collection of leaves and twigs to make 'dona' and 'patta' (plant-based utensils), herbal medicines and availability of small game. Where these forests have been destroyed to make room for commercial plantations of teak and eucalyptus, the adverse effect on the food and nutrition needs of people are apparent.

Even where natural forests remain, the fact that some of the important food items of tribals (like mahua) are now also now being procured in large amounts by industries may result in their diminishing availability as staple food. And in other cases, while adequate food may be available, increasing restrictions on tribals and villagers regarding collection of forest produce can reduce their free supply of food. Occasional reports from various parts of the country suggest that all this is actually happening on an alarming scale.

IX

Without doubt, the green revolution approach to agricultural development should be given up. The following alternative approach should be emphasised.

- Protecting vast diversity of indigenous seed varieties and organic, low-cost, ecologically protective, self-reliant, local resource based farming methods.
- Using scientific knowledge to promote the above approach and the ‹agro-ecology› approach in better ways. Priorities of farm research and extension network to be entirely changed in this direction.
- Land reforms to be implemented effectively.
- Much higher allocation for agriculture and allied activities with direct benefits to organic farmers and seed savers, seed protectors.
- Better implementation of watershed schemes with low-budget small projects implemented with close involvement of rural communities and small farmers.
- Increasing greenery in villages with emphasis on indigeneous species.

X

All these aspects should be studied in a comprehensive way so that the dangers of green revolution approach as well as availability of alternatives can be brought out more clearly.

2.2 Solve Punjab Farmers' Problems

As Punjab was selected for early introduction of green revolution and the accompanying investments and subsidies, and the state also receives more remittances from family members from abroad, there has been an exaggerated perception of farm-related prosperity in the state. The reality for many of the small and marginal farmers is that of fast increasing costs and debts as well as growing non-sustainability of technology which is highly extractive and harms environment.

A few years after the advent of the green revolution it started becoming clear that Punjab's farmers were in the grip of a severe agro-ecological crisis. Earlier, Punjab grew a wide diversity of crops and crop varieties using time respected crop rotations and mixed farming systems. These were able to exist in compatibility with local soil, water and climate conditions so that even after hundreds of years of cultivation there was no heavy stress on soil and water.

However, the green revolution technology created stress for soil and water within just one or two decades. Loss of biodiversity and narrow genetic base of crops brought by technology led to greater vulnerability to heavy damage from diseases and pests. These needed heavy use of hazardous chemical pesticides and other agro-chemicals.

High dependence on heavy and unbalanced use of chemical fertilizers depletes the fertility of land. Chemical fertilizers cannot enhance the soil's organic matter which is the key to fertility. Heavy reliance on chemical fertilizers ultimately leads to a situation where more and more of these have to be used just to maintain the existing yields at rising costs. This is precisely what appears to have happened in Punjab at a relatively early stage. For example, during the five years from 1977-78 to 1981-82, use of chemical fertilizers in Punjab shot up from 465 thousand tonnes NPK to 812 thousand tonnes NPK while the yield for the major crops increased only moderately or stagnated.

What is more, chemical fertilizers are much less suitable for tropical climate and soil compared to temperate areas. Here their contribution to pollution as well as long term damage to soil fertility is much more. The contribution of earthworms in maintaining soil fertility is also much higher in our country. The agri chemicals have been very harmful to them. Chemical sprays too destroy some other friendly insects. The deeper root growth important for preventing any deficiency of micronutrients has been hampered due to the formation of pan by chemical fertilizers.

So, it is not surprising that farmers in Punjab soon experienced rising costs and stagnant yields. The farmers' costs also increased due to over investment in mechanization. According to the Punjab State Farmers Commission, the state has double the number of tractors it requires. At the same time, farmers' returns were further eroded by exploitative practices in marketing of farm produce.

All this led all too soon to increasing economic distress of farmers resulting in high levels of indebtedness. This situation was not altered to any significant extent by farm subsidies which had very low reach-out to small farmers. For example, only 6 percent of the power subsidy in 2012-13 reached small farmers, who comprise 34 percent of the farming community in Punjab.

The increasing distress of farmers has led to thousands of suicides. A survey conducted in the most affected six districts – Bathinda, Sangrur, Mansa, Barnala, Moga and Ludhiana

– revealed that 3,507 farmers killed themselves in 2000-11. Out of these, 74 percent committed suicide due to economic distress and indebtedness. Eighty percent of these suicides were by small farmers cultivating less than five acres of land. The average debt in such cases was Rs 234,541.

According to another Census survey of Sangrur and Bathinda districts by PAU between 2000 and 2008, 1,757 farmers committed suicide – 1,288 primarily due to indebtedness. Another 469 suicides took place due to other reasons. The average size of holding in such cases was three acres and the average debt was Rs 1.15 lakh.

A significant fall in cotton productivity during 1997-2003, heavy investments on digging/deepening of borewells due to a steep fall in the groundwater table and unproductive expenditure on social ceremonies were primarily responsible for causing distress in these farming families.

A study by Bharat Kisan Union (BKU-Ekta) provided a figure of 29,776 suicides by farmers in seven districts on the basis of extrapolation of sample study results. This covered the period 2001-05. In this study, 750 suicides were documented from 70 villages. On the basis of extrapolation, it was argued that the incidence of farmers' suicides per lakh population is much higher in Punjab (154) compared to the more discussed Maharashtra (62), Andhra Pradesh (33) and Karnataka (59). However, extrapolation of data from highest suffering districts may be questionable.

Studies and reports have mentioned many heart-rending stories of extreme distress. In some cases, two or more members of a single family have committed suicide. In other cases, one suicide led to conditions in which another suicide followed. In other situations, failed suicide attempts led to hospitalization, the cost of which greatly increases the indebtedness, the original stress.

A significant number of farmers in Punjab have experienced distress and tensions despite the hype about the prosperity of green revolution areas. There is need to ensure that the problems faced by farmers of Punjab are sorted out with care and caution. No policy change which can aggravate these problems should be made. It is in this wider context that the voice of protesting farmers must be heard. Any laws considered harmful by them should not be imposed on them or on farmers in other parts of the country.

2.3 Look Beyond Current Paradigm of Development

There are several areas of India which follow the intensive green revolution path of farming, based generally on heavy use of agro-chemicals, high levels of mechanization and overexploitation of water. Among these, the best known areas are a major part of Punjab, Haryana and Western Uttar Pradesh.

This belt accounts for a very significant part of the production and government procurement of some staple foods, particularly wheat, rice and sugar. The dependence on government procurement is more direct for wheat and rice. In the case of sugar companies concentrated more in Western UP, the government plays an important role in ensuring that the staggered and frequently delayed payments to farmers are finally made.

Green revolution came to this region in the decade following its introduction in India around 1965 or so.

Hence, two generations of farmers have grown up familiar only with green revolution farming. All this has happened amid propaganda from the government and agro-business describing the green revolution as progress and the earlier farming system as backward. So, people here do not generally think of learning from traditional farming, the wisdom of their grandparents, when confronted with problems. Whatever efforts are made to find solutions are generally made within the paradigm of the green revolution.

Western UP is blessed by the Ganga-Yamuna river system, fertile soil and abundant water. But decades of growing sugarcane monocultures and the network of sugar factories and liquor distilleries supported by these monocultures have depleted and polluted water sources, threatened rivers and harmed the fertility of land. Farmers face increasing tensions. Small farmers, for whom the sugarcane payment system is more difficult and less remunerative than for big farmers, invariably suffer more. Farm workers have much less work than before. There are increasing social and communal problems as well as heavy consumption of liquor.

In Punjab, the soil has been badly depleted and organic matter lost by the heavy use of chemical fertilizers and pesticides besides the giving up of mixed farming systems combining legumes, cereals and millets. In this land of five rivers, green revolution and new unsustainable monocultures are leading to fast depletion and heavy pollution of water sources. Serious diseases and health problems are blamed on chemical pesticides and herbicides. In canal irrigated areas, there has been heavy loss of fertile land caused by waterlogging and salinity. Despite more agricultural and food subsidies flowing to green revolution areas, high incidence of suicides among farmers and farm workers continues. Liquor and drug addiction are at high levels.

Somewhat similar is the situation in Haryana. In the entire green revolution belt, costs and debts among farmers have gone up heavily. In several villages, problems are hidden by remittances from migrants in Canada, the UK and other countries as well as modern urban living fostered by these contacts. But serious problems relating to farming persist.

Hence, farmers have to come out of the thinking of seeking solutions only within the paradigm of intensive green revolution farming to which they have got used to. In particular, they should seriously examine the possibilities of social agro-ecology, ecologically protective and more diverse farming and food-processing. They must also look for more possibilities of cost reduction, self-reliance and co-operation of all sections including the landless. With their higher education and more contacts with better-off consumers in nearby big cities and even abroad, they can increase earnings by getting better price for healthy food products of GM-free organic and natural farming.

2.4 Deception Against People, Environment

Linguistic deception has been increasingly used against the interests of common people and environment protection and to advance the interests of big business – on a vast scale although in subtle and veiled ways. The most common example of this is the way in which the word 'reform' has been used, particularly in economic discourse. The general meaning of 'reform' is to improve an institution, system and practice. However, in economic discourse this word has been increasingly used to convey economic changes which mainly benefit big business interests (any other benefits, if these exist at all, are incidental).

Having defined economic reforms in these terms, a battery of so-called experts is let loose, many of them front-persons of big businesses. They claim the high moral ground of reformers and pioneers of economic reforms, pretending to be unjustly treated when governments make their rare gesture of defending the interests of common people and environment.

Similarly, the expression trade reforms is often used to justify the expansion of shrewd devices of new imperialism and multinational corporations while curbing the aspirations of local small farmers and entrepreneurs. The words agricultural reforms are increasingly used to promote the expansion of big business and multinational interests in farming and food sectors.

The expression green revolution was used to give a good and attractive name to promote the control of a few rich countries and multinational companies on world farming and food system. It was also meant to achieve an ever increasing penetration of rural areas by big business, foreign and local, at the cost of sustainability and environment, the loss of hundreds of thousands of traditional crop varieties and cultivars, a genetic holocaust, and the loss or depletion of traditional wisdom of maybe a hundred generations or more. All the dissenting voices were sought to be pushed aside by proclaiming a green revolution. Who can object to such nice words, even if they are used only to hide very harsh truths, and when big propaganda networks are there to promote mischief and deception?

Similarly, the over-centralization of milk processing, decline of local processing, decline of traditional animal breeds, promotion of urban obesity at the cost of rural nutrition, plastic packaging at the cost of milk vendor and big companies at the cost of small dairy producer come in the name of white revolution. An assault on small fisherfolk and bio-diversity protective practices comes in the name of blue revolution.

The word liberalism was used initially to convey an openness to new ideas, a very positive trait. Later, this got extended to convey a thinking which supports not just individual rights and civil liberties but free enterprise in particular. So far so good. Increasingly it was the support of free enterprise which got more emphasis and this in turn got associated with the support of big business. Later, by pre-fixing 'neo' to it, liberalism got associated more with a system of justifying plunder by big business and moving away from welfare responsibilities of the state. Yet somehow the original highly positive connotation of liberalism survived, providing a strong linguist deception for a system of plunder and injustice.

In other languages, the deception can be harsher and sharper. In Hindi, economic reform translated as 'aarthik sudhar' creates a strong first impression of something good, some really nice improvement. And the translation of neo-liberalism as 'nav-udaaervaad' takes the deception even further.

It is high time this linguist deception is challenged and opposed.

2.5 Traditional Wisdom is Extremely Important

It is well recognized that not all traditions are good. Some widespread aspects of many traditional societies like discrimination and inequality at various levels (such as caste, gender and class) need to be rejected. However, there are several other facets relating to the wisdom accumulating over centuries regarding farming and allied activities, forestry, water conservation, crafts and related issues which need to be protected and valued.

This traditional wisdom evolved from people, spread over several generations often in adverse conditions, has invaluable lessons in terms of skills and solutions specific to local conditions and needs. The skills, talents, wisdom, initiatives and efforts of so many generations are captured in traditional wisdom. We can ignore this only at our folly and at tremendous costs to our and future generations.

Traditional wisdom survived for thousands of years because one generation could inherit this from the previous generation. But what has happened more recently is that this respect and grace are increasingly missing. There is instead a tendency to uproot and displace whatever is represented in traditional wisdom and call this progress. Unfortunately, such tendencies are seen not just in most capitalist but also in several communist societies. This is a cause for concern.

In several regions, farming could be practiced for thousands of years and yet the soil health was maintained. The organic content of the soil remained, earthworms and micro-organisms of soil continued in abundance and the water balance was maintained. But as soon as traditional wisdom displaced, within a few decades, all this was badly disrupted, soil health and water abundance were gone, organic content of soil was badly ruined and earthworms perished in billions.

This realization has re-emphasized the need for protecting traditional wisdom. However, powerful authorities guided by narrow interests whose only goal is to earn money and acquire dominance are not listening. Climate scientists are telling us how important it is to protect organic content of soil not only for the already well-known reason of protecting and enhancing natural fertility of soil but also for capturing carbon, badly needed in times of climate change.

It is time to wake up and take many-sided and strong efforts to protect traditional wisdom in farming and allied activities. This is true of most human societies but all the more so of tropical countries like India which are blessed with more diverse crop varieties and which have retained agriculture as the main source of livelihood at a time when many Western countries were fast industrializing.

2.6 The Greater Green Revolution

The green revolution has been widely discussed and its different aspects have been highlighted by various observers according to their own understanding of emphasis and priorities. To this writer, the essence of the green revolution seems to be in the following tendencies. They are more significant because these seem to be shared by technological changes in other sectors of rural development spread by the same forces.

Firstly, the green revolution seeks to draw the peasantry of even very remote areas into the pressures and influences of the international market. As long as the farmer continued to grow his traditional varieties with very meager or even nil quantities of agrochemicals, diesel or machinery, he was least affected by what happened in the oil, fertilizer and other related industries of the world or by the relation of the domestic industry producing these inputs to the industry of other countries. But with the advent of the green revolution all this suddenly became quite important for millions of farmers in the form of price and availability of fertilizers, pesticides, diesel and tractors.

Secondly, the propaganda on behalf of the green revolution emphasizes its suitability for small farmers. In a technological sense, there is nothing to stop a farmer from growing new seeds. Seen in the reality of Indian rural conditions and indeed in those of many countries, the new seeds requiring expensive inputs in large amounts are most likely to trap the low-resource, poor farmer in a debt trap. Those endowed with the largest resource base in rural areas are able to take advantage of the several new opportunities, not necessarily in agricultural production but even more in trade of produce as well as inputs or 'agro business' which the green revolution seeds and their related inputs bring.

A related issue is the narrow way in which the green revolution concerns itself with the basic problem of hunger. In Indian conditions it was evident that to effectively tackle hunger, food production should not just grow but grow specifically on the fields of the poorer farmers in backward areas. On the other hand, by emphasizing concentration of resources in the already well endowed regions and at least initially in the better-off farmers the green revolution follows an opposite pattern.

By doing so it makes it possible to collect 'marketable surplus' of grain from a relatively small area to enhance the government's stocks of grain which, however, by itself cannot ensure that this food reaches the hungry. Thus, the green revolution takes a cynical view of the pain of hunger – flaunting grain stocks and asking where is the problem, while doing nothing effective by itself to really increase the ability of the hungry to eat better.

Lastly, the green revolution strategy has been promoted and supported at various levels by foundations and aid organizations based in Western countries besides the multilateral aid, finance and research organizations in which these countries are dominant. These interests have been generally very supportive of big agribusiness corporations.

If these are accepted as some of the most important features of the green revolution, the technological changes in other areas of rural dairy development, fisheries and forestry can be seen as exhibiting much the same tendencies. Hence, these overall changes can be described as the greater green revolution.

In the case of dairy development, the foreign aid-based Operation Flood project strengthened for all time to come the trend of big infrastructure, big city-supply centered path, denying a more imaginative and pioneering path more suited to the needs of India. The strategy of this project put more emphasis on the technology of crossbreed cows which is less suited for small, low resource farmer and for hot weather conditions (likely to be even less suitable for times of climate change and for meeting bullock needs of agriculture).

By emphasizing the availability of plenty of milk and milk products in cities for those who have the purchasing power, the 'white revolution' adopts a cynical attitude towards the problem of malnutrition, being concerned with only the product and not with who gets it.

As milk processing moves away from villages, the cheapest by product of 'chaach', also the cheapest source of protein, is likely to become much less available to poorer households, compared to its much more abundant and more or less free availability earlier. As more emphasis shifts to supplying milk to big cities with large-scale urban milk processing plants, crucial aspects such as improving pastures and equal deal for weaker sections in dairy development get less importance.

With oilseed processing also shifting to huge city processing, oilcakes and other nutritive feed do not go to local farm and dairy animals. These go instead to those who can pay more. In practice this often means the export market. Operation Flood established the trend of mixing fresh milk arbitrarily with cheaper stored milk powder and butter oil from any part of world. Using this, the organized dairy sector can price out the independent small dairy producer any day. The independent small dairy producer keeps complaining that her costs are more than her price in a system dominated by the organized sector which can mix milk powder and butter oil with fresh milk to always have a competitive edge over the unorganized sector and independent small farmer.

In forestry, massive aid for projects has been accompanied by increased orientation of officials towards forestry practices and policies to predominantly satisfy the need of industries. Emphasis on supporting the growth of mainly those species which industry finds useful at the expense of trees needed by tribals and other villagers has played havoc with their lives. This has specially hit their access to free food available in forests (which was specially useful in lean agricultural season and in drought years).

Forestry projects have emphasized monocultures of commercially and industrially useful species of trees with adverse impacts on environment and availability of food, fodder, medicinal plants as well as other useful forest based products to local communities, particularly tribals. This trend is harmful also for wild life and biodiversity. India's Fifth Five Year Plan stated that its priority is to shift 'to a dynamic programme of production forestry aiming at clear felling and creating large-scale man-made forests with the help of institutional financing'. A little later, the National Commission of Agriculture went to the extent of saying, 'Production of industrial wood will have to be the raison d'étre for the existence of forests.'

In the area of marine fisheries also the traditional fisher folk communities have suffered with the growing linkages of coastal fisheries to export-led growth and to the domination of big business interests and increasing mechanization, promoted by international projects and agencies. In some places, rising exports of fish have been accompanied by declining local per capita availability of this staple protein. In many places, original fishers have faced increasing difficulties while late entrants to marine fisheries have made fortunes. Aquaculture projects promoted by big business interests have faced increasing criticism for ecological ruin and adverse impacts on coastal communities.

The extension of several important features of the green revolution as also the same thinking underlying the technological changes in agriculture to other areas of rural development may be called the greater green revolution.

It is a common and important part of all aspects of the green revolution and the greater green revolution that strong attempts are made to break the self-reliance of rural communities and to increase their dependence on outside forces. In course of time this leads to indebtedness and even to displacement of rural communities from their land or other resource base. This is particularly the fate of the weaker and more vulnerable members of these communities but not confined only to them.

Thus, the greater green revolution may be defined as an extension of similar thinking and technology in animal husbandry and dairying, fisheries, forestry and other related activities which lead to a disruption of traditional practices and related wisdom, accompanied by the imposition of technologies and inputs which break self-reliance and impose exploitative linkages. These are harmful for sustainable development, nutrition, environment protection and animal welfare but lead to increased business for industrial interests.

GM Crops: A Serious Threat

There are over 500 research publications by scientists of indisputable integrity, who have no conflict of interest, that establish harmful effects of GM crops on human, animal and plant health and on environment and biodiversity. For example, a recent paper by Indian scientists showed that the Bt gene in both cotton and brinjal leads to inhibition of growth and development of the plant. On the other hand, virtually every paper supporting GM crops is by scientists who have a declared conflict of interest or whose credibility and integrity can be doubted.

—Prof Pushpa M. Bhargava

Founder of Centre for Cellular and Molecular Biology
Vice Chairperson of National Knowledge Commission

3.1 Gene Edited Crops Threaten Food Security

Amid warnings by distinguished scientists against Genetically Modified (GM) crops, a strong lobby led by some of the biggest corporate interests is using several tricks to find a way past the scientific evidence against GM crops.

Dr Pushpa M Bhargava, an internationally acclaimed authority on Genetic Engineering, was appointed by the Supreme Court as an observer in the Genetic Engineering Appraisal Committee as he was widely perceived to be an accomplished expert on this issue, that too, of the highest integrity. In addition, he was seen on the basis of his past record as a persistent defender of public interest.

It is useful and interesting to see what this senior scientist had to say about GM crops. First, he made a strong effort to break the myth created by relentless manipulation by the powerful forces trying to spread GM crops in India. According to this myth, most scientific research support GM crops.

Bhargava wrote: There are over 500 research publications by scientists of indisputable integrity, who have no conflict of interest, that establish harmful effects of GM crops on human, animal and plant health, and on environment and biodiversity. For example, a paper by Indian scientists showed that the Bt gene in both cotton and brinjal leads to inhibition of growth and development of the plant. On the other hand, virtually every paper supporting GM crops is by scientists who have a declared conflict of interest or whose credibility and integrity can be doubted.

He added: The central government departments that have been acting as peddlers of GM technology – probably in collusion with MNCs marketing GM seeds – have shown little respect for law.

In *Food Without Choice* (published in the *Tribune*) Bhargava drew pointed attention to the 'attempt by a small but powerful minority to propagate genetically modified crops to serve their interests and those of multinational corporations (read the US), the bureaucracy, the political set-up and a few unprincipled and unethical scientists and technologists who can be used as tools.'

He warned: The ultimate goal of this attempt in India, of which the leader is Monsanto, is to obtain control over Indian agriculture and thus food production. With 60 percent of our population engaged in agriculture and living in villages, this would essentially mean not only a control over our food security but also over our farmer security, agricultural security and security of the rural sector.

The strong stand of Bhargava against GM crops is supported by other eminent scientists around the world. A group of eminent scientists organized under the Independent Science Panel (ISP) has stated: GM crops have failed to deliver the promised benefits and are posing escalating problems on the farm. Transgenic contamination is now widely acknowledged to be unavoidable, and hence there can be no co-existence of GM and non-GM agriculture. Most important of all, GM crops have not been proven safe. On the contrary, sufficient evidence has emerged to raise serious safety concerns, that if ignored, could result in irreversible damage to health and environment. GM crops should be firmly rejected now.

The ISP is a panel of scientists from many disciplines and countries, committed to the promotion of science for public good. In a document titled *The case for a GMO-free Sustainable World*, it has stated: By far the most insidious dangers of genetic engineering are inherent to the process itself, which greatly enhances the scope and probability of horizontal gene transfer and recombination, the main route to creating viruses and bacteria that cause disease epidemics. This was highlighted in 2001, by the 'accidental' creation of a killer mouse virus in the course of an apparently innocent genetic engineering experiment. Newer techniques, such as DNA shuffling, are allowing geneticists to create in a matter of minutes in the laboratory millions of recombinant viruses that have never existed in billions of years of evolution. Disease-causing viruses and bacteria and their genetic material are the predominant materials and tools for genetic engineering, as much as for the intentional creation of bio weapons.

At a time when more and more people are concerned about the serious health risks and numerous adverse impacts of genetically modified (GM) crops and genetically modified organisms (GMOs), the enormously powerful GMO multinationals have tried again to introduce confusion and uncertainty in public mind by coming up with the concept of gene-edited crops. They argue that these should not be subject to the same restrictions as GM crops. However, in July 2018, the Court of Justice of the European Union (ECJ) in Luxembourg ruled that gene-edited crops should be subject to the same rules and regulations as GM crops.

Earlier, a review of the legal and scientific facts surrounding this debate by Dr Janet Cotter and Dr R

Steinbrecher (published in The Ecologist) concluded, 'It is clear that gene-edited crops and animals need to be assumed as GMOs in the same way as current GM crops.'

Gene editing researchers can add, delete or modify bits of an organism's genome. The European Court has said that any crops edited using CRISPR or other gene-editing techniques must abide by the same laws restricting the use of GMOs. More specifically, the court said that it 'considers that the risks linked to the use of these new mutagenesis techniques might prove to be similar to those that result from production and release of a GMO through trans-genesis since the direct modification of the genetic material of an organism through mutagenesis makes it possible to obtain the same effects as the introduction of foreign gene into the organism (trans-genesis) and these new techniques make it possible to introduce genetically modified varieties at a rate out of all proportion to those resulting from the application of conventional methods of mutagenesis.'

Welcoming the verdict, Franziska Achterberg, Greenpeace EU's Food Policy Director, said: Releasing these new GMOs into the environment without proper safety measures is illegal and irresponsible, particularly given that gene editing can lead to unintended side-effects.... The European Commission and the European governments must now ensure that all new GMOs are fully tested and labeled, and that any field trials are brought under GMO rules.

The Friends of the Earth said: We applaud the European Court of Justice for this forward-looking decision.

There is a need for a lot of caution in India as powerful

interests are promoting the possibilities of introduction of several GM food crops. They are also trying to use gene-editing as a means of getting approval.

3.2 Can GM Crops Cause Mass Discontent?

Strong pressures are being exerted to somehow get GM crops approved. Efforts are on to get the moratorium on Bt brinjal lifted so that the path can be cleared for subsequent approval of several other GM (genetically modified or genetically engineered) crops, including staple food crops like rice.

It is important to warn that GM crops can lead to mass distress followed by mass discontent. This will become evident to anyone who follows the available scientific literature and other reports on the performance of GM crops and genetic engineering.

Let us first look at what GM crops can do to farmers. The Independent Science Panel (ISP) said after examining all aspects of GM crops: GM crops have failed to deliver the promised benefits and are posing escalating problems on the farm. Transgenic contamination is now widely acknowledged to be unavoidable, and hence there can be no co-existence of GM and non-GM agriculture. Most important of all, GM crops have not been proven safe. On the contrary, sufficient evidence has emerged to raise serious safety concerns, that if ignored could result in irreversible damage to health and the environment. GM crops should be firmly rejected now.

How can our government ignore such clear scientific opinion on the hazards of GM crops provided by eminent scientists? What this statement says is that GM crops are not safe and these can contaminate all other normal crops as well. In other words, all farmers will be affected by these hazardous crops. Even farmers who reject GM crops will have to face the hazards.

This threat becomes serious and of a permanent nature when we remember that it is almost impossible to fully recall GM crops which have been released once. As Professor Susan Bardocz noted, '**GM is the first irreversible technology in human history. When a GMO (Genetically Modified Organism) is released, it is out of our control; we have no means to call it back....** Since GMOs are self-replicating, releasing them might have dire consequences for human and animal health and for the environment and can change evolution.'

More recently, 17 distinguished scientists from Europe, the US, Canada and New Zealand wrote to the Prime Minister of India warning against 'the unique risks (of GM crops) to food security, farming systems and bio-safety impacts which are ultimately irreversible.' This letter added: The GM transformation process is highly mutagenic leading to disruptions to host plant genetic structure and function, which in turn leads to disturbances in the biochemistry of the plant. This can lead to novel toxin and allergen production as well as reduced/altered nutrition quality.

The US is the leading country growing GM crops. There are several stories of distress and harassment American farmers have suffered due to GM crops and the companies promoting them. Words like 'Franken seeds' are used to describe the harmful unpredictable crops while 'seed police' denotes the aggressive men sent to regulate family farmers.

But this is nothing compared to the mass distress and discontent that can result in India where nearly 60 percent people are involved in farming and related activities. One can imagine what will happen when so many farmers are exposed to the threat of genetic contamination, apart from being squeezed into a situation where many have no option but to regularly buy expensive seeds of a few companies which control the market.

Vested interests have spread the wrong notion that genetic engineering holds the promise of greatly increasing farm yields. According to the report by the Independent Science Panel, the consistent finding from independent research and on-farm surveys since 1999 is that GM crops have failed to deliver the promised benefits of significantly increasing yields or reducing herbicide and pesticide use. 'GM crops have cost the United States an estimated $12 billion in farm subsidies, lost sales and product recalls due to transgenic contamination.... The instability of transgenic lines has plagued the industry from the beginning, and this may be responsible for a string of major crop failures'.

Above all, if the crops are widely believed to be hazardous, won't people try to avoid them? This will certainly affect the domestic as well as the export markets.

In his widely acclaimed book '*Genetic Roulette*', Jeffrey M Smith has summarised the results of a lot of research on the health hazards of GM crops/food. Lab animals tested with GM foods had stunted growth, impaired immune systems, bleeding stomachs, abnormal and potentially precancerous cell growth in the intestines, impaired blood cell development, misshapen cell structures in the liver, pancreas and testicles, altered gene expression and cell metabolism, liver and kidney lesions, partially astrophied livers, inflamed kidneys, less developed brains and testicles, enlarged livers, pancreas and intestines, reduced digestive enzymes, higher blood sugar, inflamed lung tissue, increased death rates and higher offspring mortality.

Michael Antoniou, a molecular geneticist at King's College, London, says: If the kind of detrimental effects seen in animals fed GM food were observed in a clinical setting, the use of the product would have been halted and further research instigated to determine the cause and find possible solutions. However, what we find repeatedly in the case of GM food is that both governments and industry plough on ahead with the development, endorsement and marketing (of) GM foods despite the warnings of potential ill health from animal feeding studies, as if nothing has happened. This is to the point where governments and industry even seem to ignore the results of their own research!

Bhargava explains how Indian farmers will suffer if GM crops like Bt brinjal are allowed to spread in the country. Eighty-four percent of our farmer community consists of small or marginal farmers with a holding of less than four hectares land. According to Monsanto data, Bt brinjal pollen can travel for 30 metres and could thus easily contaminate the neighbouring non-Bt brinjal field. In course of time, we would be left with no non-Bt yield even if the farmers do not want the transgenic crop. Unlike in Europe, Britain and many other countries, India has few labeling laws. In these countries, any food product which has more than 0.9 percent of GM material must be labelled as genetically modified item. Therefore, we would neither be able to export our vegetables stock nor exercise choice with regard to GM brinjal or a non-GM brinjal. There is an ever-increasing demand everywhere, including our country, for organically grown food which fetches the farmer better price. This market will also be lost with the introduction of GM foods.

In addition, there is the ethical dilemma faced by vegetarians who may find it difficult to select food when animal genes are introduced into plant genes. The choice becomes even more difficult (and not just for vegetarians) when even human genes are introduced into food crops. This dilemma is most difficult to resolve when GM foods are not specifically labelled. In fact GM food companies try their best to avoid any legal requirement of specific labelling of GM food.

As genetic engineering is all about transferring genes from one species to another entirely unrelated species, these are all sorts of possibilities of playing havoc with the religious sentiments and emotions of people. There was an obnoxious example of transferring human genes into pigs; there are other equally weird examples.

The extent to which genetic engineering is playing havoc with nature is evident from this quote from *Genetic Roulette*, 'Spider genes were inserted into goat DNA, in hopes that the goat milk would contain spider web protein for use in bullet-proof vests. Cow genes turned pig skin into cowhides. Jellyfish genes lit up pigs' noses in the dark.

Arctic fish genes gave tomatoes and strawberries tolerance to frost.'

Notice particularly the words 'Cow genes turned pig skin into cowhides'. In India cow is considered holy by some communities while pig is considered the opposite by others (all this at the level of religious sentiments). So what do you say about a technology which thinks nothing of turning 'pig skin into cowhides'?

3.3 Genetic Engineering Increasingly Questioned

In agriculture and animal husbandry in particular, genetic engineering has far reaching implications as it allows the introduction into plants and animals of entirely new characteristics, including genes originally found in unrelated plants, animals or micro-organisms. This is very different from traditional breeding practices.

The technology is spreading so fast that very adverse consequences can result even before we get to understand the implications. At a very early stage of its development, this technology has got heavily concentrated in the hands of a few giant corporations which want to commercially exploit it to reap profits. In the process, critics fear, serious and irreversible damage can be caused to environment, to food system and to the health of millions.

In 1994, several scientists studying the impact of genetic engineering got together at the International Conference on Redefining of Life Sciences at Penang, Malaysia, by the Third World Network. They issued a statement (Penang Statement) which questioned the scientific basis of genetic engineering. The statement said:

The new biotechnology based upon genetic engineering makes the assumption that each specific feature of an organism is encoded in one or a few specific, stable genes so that the transfer of these genes results in the transfer of a discrete feature. This extreme form of genetic reductionism has already been rejected by the majority of biologists and many other members of the intellectual community because it fails to take into account the complex interactions between genes and their cellular, extracellular and external environments that are involved in the development of all traits.

It has thus been impossible to predict the consequences of transferring a gene from one type of organism to another in a significant number of cases. The limited ability to transfer identifiable molecular characteristics between organisms through genetic engineering does not constitute the demonstration of any comprehensive or reliable system for predicting all the significant effects of transposing genes.

In a widely quoted paper, *The Biotechnology Bubble,* Dr Mae-Wan Ho (who heads Bio-Electrodynamics Lab of the Open University in the UK), Joe Cummins (Professor Emeritus of Genetics in Canada) and Hartmut Meyer summarised the results of several experiments, trials and commercial releases of GMOs. They write, 'There are many signs of the problems caused in genetic engineering organisms. For every product that reaches the market, there are perhaps 20 or more that fail. It is particularly disastrous for animal welfare.'

- The 'superpig' engineered with human growth hormone gene turned out arthritic, ulcerous, blind and impotent.

- The 'supersalmon' engineered, again, to grow as fast as possible, with genes belonging to other fish, ended up with big monstrous heads and died from not being able to see, breathe or feed properly.
- The latest clones of the transgenic sheep Dolly are abnormal and eight times as likely to die at birth compared with ordinary lambs.
- Even products that reach the market are failing, including crops that have been widely planted.

The authors of this paper (published in the *Ecologist*) concluded: It is important to realise that the failures are not just teething problems. They are very much the result of a reductionist science and a hit or miss technology. The transgenic foods created are unwholesome because they involve stressing the developmental and metabolic system of organisms out of balance. There are bound to be unintended effects including toxins and allergens, which current risk assessments are designed to conceal rather than reveal. The major problem is the instability of transgenic lines.

Marcello Buiatti, Plants Genetics Dept, University of Florence, warned in an essay, *GMOs-Facts and Fiction*, 'Far from being the new science, which will solve all the problems of humanity in a short time, present day genetic engineering is based on obsolete knowledge and an equally obsolete and wrong conception of life.'

Cesare Gessler of The ETH Swiss Federal Institute of Technology also expressed concern. 'The products of genetic engineering today are still at the level of a dinosaur technology. We use genes, which are foreign to a species, not knowing where they are inserted or what else will change in the whole chain from gene to protein.'

Dr Peter Wills, a theoretical biologist at Auckland University, has noted, 'By transferring genes across species barriers, which have existed for eons between species like humans and sheep, we risk breaching natural thresholds against unexpected biological processes. For example, an incorrectly folded form of an ordinary cellular protein can under certain circumstances be replicative and give rise to infectious neurological disease.'

Robert Mann, a biochemist in the same university, says, 'The gene-manipulators claim they can foresee the evolutionary results of their artificial transposing of human genes into sheep, bovine genes into tomatoes, altered bacterial genes into eggplant. But such claims are a reflection more of arrogance than of scientific analysis.'

3.4 Can Normal Crops Co-exist With GM Crops?

One factor that has not received adequate attention is that due to the threat of contamination, it is difficult for normal or organic crops to remain free from the impact of GM crops once the latter have been released.

As worldwide concern for food safety grows, it is likely that there will be increasing demand for organically grown crops and crops which are not contaminated by GM crops. One will be surrendering premium world markets if we allow our crops to be contaminated. This is why organisations like those of rice exporters have also got involved in the campaigns against GM crops. Star Link (corn engineered to contain a Bt toxin pesticide) was planted on less than 0.5% of US corn acereage. Its recall cost hundreds of millions of dollars. Even then the recall was not entirely successful.

The Independent Science Panel (ISP) has also warned against the serious threat of contamination by GM crops. Extensive transgenic contamination has occurred in maize landraces growing in remote regions in Mexico despite an official moratorium that has been in place since 1998. High levels of contamination have since been found in Canada. In a test of 33 samples of certified canola (oilseed rape) seed stocks, 32 were found contaminated. New research shows that transgenic pollen, wind-blown and deposited elsewhere, or fallen directly to the ground, is a major source of transgenic contamination. Contamination is generally acknowledged to be unavoidable, hence there can be no co-existence of transgenic and non-transgenic crops.

ISP added, 'Crops engineered with 'suicide' genes for male sterility have been promoted as a means of 'containing'... the spread of transgenes. In reality, the hybrid crops sold to farmers spread both male sterile suicide genes as well herbicide tolerance genes via pollen.'

It is due to the serious threat of contamination that even trials of GM crops are considered unacceptably risky.

Prominent environmentalist Sailendra Nath Ghosh has written: In view of the virtual impossibility of preventing contamination, even the open-field trials ought not to have been permitted. According to independent geneticists, the isolation distance needed to be both in time and space. The land on which the GM crop is to be grown should not sow a crop in the previous or succeeding year. Cross-pollinating crops, unlike the self-pollinating ones, require isolation distance of three to four kms. The implementation of these requirements is impossible under Indian conditions. Farmers would not keep their lands fallow. Crops in adjoining fields are almost always planted up to the boundaries. The trials needed to be in greenhouses controlled by independent institutions.

Several of these threats were examined at the international conference, The Penang Statement which listed a wide range of potential adverse effects of genetic engineering. Of particular concern is the difficulty or impossibility of recalling GEOs which have been released into the environment or which have escaped from containment.

The potential ecological risks of applying genetic engineering to agriculture include the possibility that some transgenic crops could become noxious weeds. Others could become a conduit through which new genes may move to wild plants which themselves could then become weeds. The new weeds could adversely affect farm crops as well as wild ecosystems. Similarly, genetically engineered fish, shellfish and insects could become pests under certain conditions.

Plants are presently being engineered to contain parts of a virus in order to become virus-resistant. Some scientists have raised the possibility that widespread use of transgenic virus-resistant plants in agriculture may lead to new strains of viruses or allow a virus to infect a new host. There are concerns that the creation of new viral strains and the broadening of the virus' host may increase the risks of new viral diseases that adversely affect crops and other plants. Mechanisms have been described whereby genetically engineered plants could plausibly give rise to new plant diseases.

The Penang Statement warned that the rapid spread of transgenic crops poses a threat to traditional crop varieties and wild plants that are the major sources of crop genetic diversity. Some traits of organisms may take decades or even longer to manifest themselves. An organism declared 'safe' in the short term could eventually prove to be dangerous.

Another ecological risk is the possibility that field or forestry plants engineered to express toxic substances like pesticides and pharmaceutical drugs may poison certain non-target organisms. Transgenes for insecticidal or fungicidal compounds introduced into crops to inhibit pests may unintentionally kill non-target and beneficial insects and fungi. Transgenic crops used to manufacture drugs or industrial oils and chemicals could potentially harm animals, insects and soil microorganisms.

A possible chemical contamination of surface and ground water by microorganisms or plants with unusual or accelerated metabolic processes is a special concern because of the crucial importance of water for all life. It may be impossible to recall and difficult to control harmful GEOs, especially those that may contaminate ground water.

The statement warned that developing countries in particular face special risks. 'Third World countries face even greater environmental risks than countries of the North because, in contrast, they have many wild relatives of many crops and thus there are more opportunities for various kinds of rogue species to be created.'

Moreover, most Third World countries have less scientific expertise and legal or regulatory capacity to monitor, assess and control activities involving genetically engineered organisms and are thus even more vulnerable to adverse impacts.

This issue should be examined in the context of what has been called the 'terminator technology'. In a widely discussed paper (published in the *Ecologist*), Ricarda A Steinbrecker, Science Director of the Genetics Forum UK, and Pat Roy Mooney (widely acclaimed winner of the Right to Livelihood Award) summarise the implications of this controversial use of genetic engineering.

On March 3, 1998, the US Department of Agriculture (USDA) and a little-known cotton-seed enterprise called Delta and Pine Land Company acquired US patent 5,723,765 or the Technology Protection System (TPS). Within days, the rest of the world knew TPS as Terminator Technology. Its declared goal is to promulgate plants that will produce self-terminating offspring - suicide seeds. Terminator Technology epitomises what the genetic engineering of food crops is all about and gives an insight into the driving forces behind the corporate campaign to control and own life.

The paper says, 'Most alarming though is the possibility that the Terminator genes themselves could infect the agricultural gene pool of the neighbour's crops and of wild and weedy relatives, placing a time bomb. Temporary "gene silencing" of the poison gene or failed activation of the Terminator countdown enables such infection.'

Evidently, the threat from GM crops to natural farming systems and environment is so serious that a commercial release cannot be allowed. Even experimental trials should be asked to wait till definite ways to avoid hazards can be found.

3.5 Can Genetic Engineering Increase Crop Yields?

That genetically engineered crops pose a major threat to safety and environment is widely recognised now. Despite this the companies involved in their spread make a strong plea for these crops claiming that the yield from them can be much higher. What these companies say time and again is that in order to meet the food needs of a growing population, one has to increase yield and this can be done only or predominantly by spreading genetically engineered crops. This claim is false as there is no basis for concluding that these crops can give better yields on a sustainable basis.

The Independent Science Panel (ISP) has made it clear that genetically modified crops have failed to deliver the promised significantly increasing yields or reducing herbicide and pesticide use.

A Friends of the Earth report (2008), *Who Benefits From GM Crops?* says that genetic engineering has been at best neutral with respect to yield. At the macro level, average cotton yields have stagnated since the adoption of Bt cotton in the US as in other countries like Argentina, Australia and Colombia.

In April 2009, the Union of Concerned Scientists (UCS) published a report, *Failure to Yield*, confirming that 'after 20 years of research and 13 years of commercialisation, GM crops have failed to increase yields' and that 'traditional breeding outperforms genetic engineering hands down'.

In some cases, the yields for a short initial period were indeed high, creating a rush for the new seeds. But after some time such expectations could not be maintained. On the other hand, there are many examples of farmers who invested their meagre resources and borrowed heavily to buy expensive GM seeds and other supporting inputs (for example herbicides linked to these seeds) but felt betrayed as the low yield left them saddled with debts. There were reports of suicides by such farmers. There have been allegations of GM crops like Bt cotton being introduced in rainfed areas like those of Vidarbha (India) for which these were not suited.

In the case of Monsanto's 1997 Roundup-resistant cotton crop it was reported that the cotton balls drop off when sprayed with Roundup. Farmers in seven states in the US sought compensation for losses.

'A number of different viral-resistant transgenic plants engineered with a viral gene actually showed increased propensity to generate new, often super-infectious viruses by recombination. There is widespread instability of transgenic lines; they generally do not breed true,' said a paper, *The Biotechnology Bubble*.

The paper says:

- In a field trial of Bt-cotton in Thailand, 30 percent of the bees around the test fields died.
- Unilever used tissue culture techniques to regenerate oil palms in Malaysia years ago. This has now been abandoned as many plants aborted in the field or failed to flower.

Kavitha Kuruganti points out in a paper, *Bt Cotton and the Myth of Enhanced Yield*, that the 2008 yields of US soybean (at 40 bushels per acre, as per National Agricultural Statistics Service of USDA) with 92 percent of such soybean being genetically modified are lower than the 1994 yields of 41.4 bushels before GM soybean was introduced. 'It is important to note that the 1996-2000 period saw a sharp decline in yield growth in cotton – the period when GM cotton increased to 61 percent of total cotton cultivation in the US.'

A University of Nebraska study found that Roundup Ready GM soya varieties yielded 5 percent less than their closest conventional relatives and 10 percent less than high-yielding conventional lines. This implies a loss in a production of nearly 200 kg/Ha.

A study by Barney Gordon (2007) (published in Better Crops) found in the context of Roundup Ready soya varieties that glyphosate applied to the GM crop was inhibiting the uptake of nutrients like manganese essential to plant health and performance.

Dr Jack A Heinemann of the School of Biological Sciences, University of Canterbury, Christchurch, New Zealand, has a decade-long experience of reviewing safety information from companies on their genetically engineered crops. He writes, 'The Bt trait does not increase yield, it is just becoming nearly impossible to source the best varieties without the Bt transgenes.'

Why is this so? Dr Heinemann answers, 'The yield benefit (in Bt cotton) comes from the use of high yielding hybrids that are only available as GM varieties because genetic engineering companies like Mansanto control a large proportion of the seed supply and only offer them as GM cotton varieties.'

This is confirmed by PV Satheesh, Convener of South Against Genetic Engineering, 'The final nail in the coffin of non-Bt cotton cultivation was hammered in 2006 when the industry-by forming a corporate seed cartel-successfully threw out all non-Bt cotton seeds from the market, firmly shutting out all options for farmers except the cultivation of Bt cotton.'

Heinemann asks, 'Where is the data that these same high yield varieties lacking the Bt trait and grown using sustainable techniques such as integrated pest management and agroecology perform less than GM varieties?' He answers, 'There is none at all to my knowledge, while there is evidence that GM varieties undermine sustainable agriculture.'

In Gujarat, while yields of cotton have increased significantly in recent years, this is mainly due to the impact of good weather and improvements in water and moisture conservation and irrigation. In any case, the increase in yield based on the control of high yielding seeds by a few companies should not be confused with any claims of yields relating to Bt trait or genetic engineering.

Heinemann writes, 'The yields of Bt cotton in the US… have not been consistently or sustainably higher than cotton produced using high yield varieties that were not genetically engineered, and GM varieties have contributed to financial losses for farmers. The high costs of genetically engineered seeds put farmers at financial risk.'

He concludes, 'Does India want to export control of its food? Then go with genetic engineering. If India wants to feed itself, then go with proven but so far neglected approaches that work, such as agro ecology.'

In the very first year of Bt cotton's commercial cultivation in India (2002-03), the Andhra Pradesh Department of Agriculture studied 3,709 farmers growing this Bt cotton. As many as 71 percent reported low yields.

In Madhya Pradesh, the average yield of cotton between 1996-2002 (before the introduction of Bt cotton) was 612.7 kg/Ha. In the six years after Bt cotton came in, the average cotton yield was reduced to 518.3 kg/Ha.

Above all, given the high hazards, risks and uncertainties associated with GM crops, these can never be sustainable. Markets and consumers of several countries simply do not accept GM crops.

In the letter written to the Prime Minister of India, 17 distinguished scientists from four countries pointed out that the claims relating to higher yield and protection of environment made for GM crops are absolutely false. Due to various problems of GM crops, their spread has been highly limited. This letter says:

'More than 95 percent of all GM crops are engineered to either synthesize an insecticide (Bt toxin) or to tolerate a broad-spectrum herbicide (e.g. Roundup, Liberty) or both.

'To date there are only four major commercialised GM crops (soya, maize/corn, cotton, canola/oilseed rape) most of which (soya, corn, canola) are used primarily as animal feed. All were commercialised in the late 90s. Since then, no other commercially viable GM crop application has made it to the market, especially due to farmers not accepting other GM crops (such as wheat, potatoes, and rice) for negative economic reasons (lack of buyers, loss of export markets).

'GM crops have not been widely accepted around the world. 95 percent of all GM food crops are grown in only five countries: the US, Canada, Australia, Argentina and Brazil. If you include fibre crops (cotton), India and China would be included. Only one GM crop is approved for cultivation within the European Union, MON810 corn, which has been banned by several member states invoking documented health and especially environmental risks.

'...The basic problem is that GM as employed in agriculture is conceptually flawed, crude, imprecise and poorly controlled technology, that is incapable of generating plants that contain the required multiple, coordinately regulated genes that work in an integrated way to respond to environmental challenges.

'...GM has not increased yield potential. Yields from GM crops to date have been no better and in the case of GM soya have been consistently lower. A 2009 report reviewing more than 20 academic studies clearly shows that the cultivation of GM herbicide-tolerant soybeans has not increased yields. Insect-resistant corn, meanwhile, has at best only improved yields marginally. This report found that increase in yields for both crops over the last 13 years was due to traditional breeding or improvements in agricultural practices.

'...GM crops have led to vast increases in pesticide use, not decreases and therefore reduction of agricultural pollution cannot be claimed.

'...Climate change brings sudden, extreme and unpredictable changes in weather, which requires that a cropping system be flexible, resilient and as genetically diverse as possible. GM technology offers just the opposite.

'...Stability of productivity and production is much lower with many of the GM crops commercialised today. Herbicide tolerant GM soya is far more sensitive to heat or drought stress than conventional soya.

'...GM crops are designed to be used in conjunction with synthetic pesticides and fertilisers, which are manufactured from oil and natural gas.

'GM crops do not reduce greenhouse gas emissions.

Recent data from the US Department of Agriculture has shown a vast increase in herbicide use since the introduction of GM crops tolerant to the application of these agrochemicals.

'Therefore, the introduction of GM crops has exacerbated rather than reduced agriculture's carbon footprint and is clearly unsustainable.

'Alternative proven technologies that can reduce the amount of fossil fuel used in farming already exist. This includes methods for reducing fertiliser applications, selecting farm machinery appropriate for each task, managing soil for conservation, limiting irrigation and (using) agro-ecological farming techniques.'

While the record of GM and particularly Bt varieties in increasing yields on a sustainable basis is highly suspect, safer alternatives are certainly available. As Bhargava pointed out, the Indian Council of Agricultural Research (ICAR) had not only favourably tested Integrated Pest management and bio-pesticides on 85 crops but also compiled as many as 4,000 traditional agricultural practices of which several had been validated and revalidated. Giving the example of Andhra Pradesh where at least one lakh acres are under organic farming, he said the yields here are equal to those farms of Punjab and Maharashtra where Bt varieties are being grown.

According to the *Economic Times* (Feb 13, 2020), cotton growers are rejecting non-Bt seeds. The trend is evident from the last two kharif seasons which saw revival in demand of conventional hybrids against genetically modified bt seeds.

'We have seen off-take of 7,000 kg of traditional varieties from our end which is significantly higher than previous years,' said Vijay Kumar, head of a cotton research center at Surat. According to him, climate too has played a major role in bringing about a change in preferences. The five-six preceding monsoons were good and pest attack was under control. The last two monsoons were erratic and there was a major attack of mealy bug which has changed the mindset of farmers.

Citing the example of Vidarbha in Maharashtra, he said farmers went for bt sowing there and suffered major losses due to scanty rainfall. Vidarbha depends heavily on monsoons for irrigation and scanty monsoons in the last two years led farmers to incur heavy losses. These forced many of them to commit suicide.

Rambhai Patel, a farmer at Jivapura near Himmatnagar in Gujarat's Sabarkantha district, said he stopped sowing Bt seed from kharif 2009 and has now opted for Sankar variety.

'Between 2004 and 2007, bt variety offered tremendous results but since the last two years it has failed to yield profits. Our production has been decreasing since last two seasons and so I have abandoned bt seeds,' he said. In the long run, the land loses fertility and farmer incurs heavy losses, he added. According to Patel, Bt seed have been losing resistance to ballworm, a major pest scourge in Gujarat.

3.6 Caution Ignored While introducing GM crops?

People wonder why GM crops spread in the US though several scientists (in addition to farmers and activists) have opposed GMOs there as well. An idea of the various forces responsible for this can be had from a complaint the US Securities and Exchange Commission filed in the US courts stating that a leading GMO company bribed 140 officials in 1997-2000 to obtain environmental clearances for its products. The company admitted this charge and paid a penalty of $1.5 million.

Jeffrey M Smith has explained how safety reports were prepared. The quotation below is from his *Genetic Roulette*, a book which has been recommended widely by experts. Smith writes: The industry-funded studies have become notorious for using creative ways to avoid finding problems. They feed older animals instead of more sensitive young ones, keep sample sizes too low to achieve the statistical significance needed for proof in scientific studies, dilute the GM component of the feed, overcook samples, compare results with irrelevant controls, choose obsolete insensitive detection methods, limit the duration of feeding trials, and even ignore animal deaths and sickness.

This opinion on the poor quality of studies is endorsed by others. Erik Millstone, Professor of Science Policy at the University of Sussex, commented, 'The fundamental problem of the way in which GM foods have been approved is that they haven't really been tested properly at all. All that has happened is something which I would characterize as an exercise in wishful thinking.'

But what is even more important is that when scientists spoke against GM crops, their voice was stifled using several unethical ways. Jeffrey Smith reports in the context of the experiences in the US, where GM crops have spread the most. The FDA (Food and Drug Administration) was fully aware that GM crops were meaningfully different. That, in fact, was the overwhelming consensus among the technical experts in the agency. The scientists agreed that genetic engineering leads to 'different risks' than traditional breeding and had repeatedly warned their superiors that GM foods might create unpredictable, hard-to-detect side effects.

The scientists' concerns were kept secret in 1992 when FDA policy was put into place. But seven years later, internal records were made public due to a lawsuit and the deception came to light. The agency's newly released 44,000 pages revealed that government scientists' 'references to the unintended negative effects… were progressively deleted from drafts of the policy statement (over the protests of agency scientists'. They further revealed that 'the FDA was under orders from the White House to promote GM crops and that Michael Taylor, Monsanto's former attorney and later its Vice President, was brought into the FDA to oversee policy development. With Taylor in charge, the scientists' warnings were ignored and denied'.

The story of the UK is no less shocking, adds Smith. In the mid-1990s, the UK government commissioned scientists to develop an assessment protocol for GM crop approvals that would be used in the UK and eventually by the EU. In 1998, three years into the project, the scientists discovered that potatoes engineered to produce a harmless insecticide caused extensive health damage to rats. The pro-GM government immediately cancelled the project, the lead scientist was fired and the research team dismantled.

It is due to the likely use of unfair means to speed up highly hazardous introduction of GMOs that citizens need to be vigilant on this issue which affects food security, livelihoods and environment.

According to the Independent Science Panel, there has been a history of misrepresentation and suppression of scientific evidence, especially on horizontal gene transfer. Key experiments failed to be performed or were performed badly and then misrepresented. Many experiments were not followed up, including investigations on whether the CaMV 35S promoter is responsible for the 'growth factor-like' effects observed in young rats fed GM potatoes.

Coming to the more recent debate on Bt brinjal, Bhargava, nominated by the Supreme Court in the Genetic Engineering Approval Committee (GEAC), pointed out that when Monsanto's dossier containing all the bio-safety tests it had done was put in the public domain in 2009, there were serious criticisms by many scientists from around the world.

Bhargava's criticism centered around the following points:

- A large body of concerned, knowledgeable and reputed scientists has agreed that some 30 or so tests need to be done before a GM plant is cleared for environmental release. Monsanto had done less than 10.
- Even these tests were done largely by Monsanto. There is no facility in the country to determine whether the tests were actually done.
- There were many scientific errors even in the tests done by Monsanto.

The GEAC appointed a committee (EC-II) to prepare a report on such criticism. But Bhargava and others were essentially given just one day to review the 102-page report. Still, thanks to his vast experience he could see that there were 'internal inconsistencies in the report, inconsistencies between the report and the earlier data that had been put in public domain and outright scientific absurdities'.

When Bhargava sought time for a review meeting of eminent experts, the request was ignored. The GEAC gave its hurried approval to Bt brinjal.

This is just one example of several arbitrary, unjustified, hurried approvals given to GM crops.

Scientists from the US, Canada, Europe and New Zealand wrote to India's Prime Minister:

'India's regulators do not require independent bio-safety tests but uncritically accept as evidence of safety research conducted by the company applying for commercial clearance of the product. This raises serious questions regarding impartiality and conflicts of interest, which are clearly justified, based on published evidence of bias in the research conducted by industry that is contrary to accepted normal scientific conduct.

'Experimental design used by the applicant is flawed, almost invariably containing irrelevant "control" non-GM comparator crop varieties, which serve to mask rather than to isolate and reveal the effect of the GM transformation process.

'The biological testing required is not adequate to detect either acute or chronic toxic effects of GM foods. At best, only 90-day feeding studies are required by the government's SOPs without an obligatory requirement for toxicological and histological evaluation. In order to assess medium and long-term (life-long) health impacts it is necessary to conduct lifetime and multigenerational feeding studies. Only these will reliably determine fertility and chronic health impacts, which is essential because it is the intention that people will be eating GM foods for their whole lifetime.

'Experimental data is invariably not made publicly available for independent scientific scrutiny under the pretext of commercial confidentiality. This has required court action (both in Europe and India) in order to obtain the information needed to assess the quality of the research submitted by industry to be scrutinised by authoritative bio-safety experts. Such independent re-evaluation of submitted industry data has repeatedly found that this research and its interpretation thereof to be flawed, inadequate, biased and thus misleading.'

A group of 24 eminent citizens of India wrote to the Prime Minister:

'We must conclude that there has been a purposeful and systematic intent by the regulators (GEAC, RCGM and DBT) to mislead you and former Prime Ministers about the truth of GM crops. We are furthermore convinced by the evidence on record of a blatant conflict of interest within the regulators and the committee charged with the appraisal of Bt brinjal called the Bt brinjal Expert Committee II (EC-II). The evidence also shows that the appraisal process, minimal guidelines used and subsequent approval are fraudulent.

'Information just received under the RTI squarely refutes the regulator's claim that the extensive reports from several states in India of allergenicity and specifically, animal deaths from toxic reactions attributed to grazing in Bt cotton fields have no substance. This is a serious falsification of the true facts. No investigation of any depth, leave alone of scientific rigour, has been conducted to ascertain the safety of the Bt gene in Bt cotton and the reason for the animal deaths. We quite simply have not done the studies. Moreover, we do not have the means to test for allergenic reactions to Bt toxins.

'Unfortunately, the Minister of Agriculture, Sharad Pawar, even allegedly saw fit to bring inappropriate pressure on the Chairperson of the Committee and interfere with the regulatory process. It is deeply worrying that Monsanto is also in a position to influence the regulatory process in India. Monsanto has been indicted for and convicted of serious crimes for repeated fraudulent processes and procedures in safety-testing of GM crops and is presently under investigation by the US Justice Department for antitrust law violations. '

According to a cover story in *Tehelka*, the GEAC in January 2008 cited reports from the Indian Veterinary Research Institute (IVRI) and the Andhra Animal Husbandry Department to show 'conclusive proof of safety' to animals from Bt cotton feed. But when Anthra, a veterinary research organisation, filed an RTI with the IVRI asking for a copy of the report, the institute responded that 'no studies had been done by them and that the IVRI had not submitted any reports to the GEAC'.

Dr Sagari R Ramdas, Co-Director of Anthra, wrote that since 2005, shepherds and farmers from different parts of India, particularly Andhra Pradesh, Haryana, Karnataka and Maharashtra, have reported their cattle falling sick after grazing on genetically modified cotton or they were fed Bt cotton seeds; in some instances they died.

Despite several reports and representations to regulatory and research institutions at various levels, there was a persistent reluctance amongst the scientific establishment to respond, investigate and research the core issue. The reaction of the establishment was bureaucratic and dismissive.

Ramdas added, 'Shepherds unambiguously declared that their animals, which had never died or fallen sick while being grazed on regular cotton fields since the past 10 years, began to exhibit morbid changes when grazed on the GM crop.

'In Haryana, there was a strong correlation between feeding Bt cotton seeds and cotton seed cake to milch animals, and drop in milk yield and several reproductive disorders such as prolapse of uterus, premature birth of calves, increase in the incidence of abortions and decrease in conception rate.'

3.7 Why Moratorium on Bt Brinjal Should Continue?

On February 9, 2010, Jairam Ramesh, India's Union Minister for Environment and Forests, announced a moratarium on Bt brinjal which was widely welcomed – not just in India but globally – on grounds of health, environment and safety. However, a relatively small but extremely powerful section of vested interests set in motion high-power efforts to remove this moratorium.

To give an idea of how strong these vested interests are, we may mention two facts. Firstly, some influential politicians and technocrats have been behaving as though they are brokers or employees of these vested interests. Secondly, the MNC which most visibly represents these interests has got away so far with the most shocking unethical practices, including large-scale bribery, to get its highly harmful products/crops approved.

So those fighting for safety, health and environment protection have to initiate an even bigger effort to counter these forces. This can start with the excellent document Jairam Ramesh released while announcing the moratorium.

The Minister stated how widespread the opposition to Bt brinjal was. 'All states which have written to me have expressed apprehension on Bt brinjal and have called for extreme caution.' As the subject 'is extremely important in our federal framework and agriculture is a state subject', he summarised the views of the state governments.

Andhra Pradesh: It is clear that the data generated, the tests conducted and the information disseminated by GEAC are not sufficient for suggesting the commercial release of Bt brinjal... Until safety parameters in terms of environment, human and animal health are clearly established, release of Bt brinjal for commercial cultivation is to be deferred.

Kerala: Government of Kerala has taken a decision to prohibit all environmental release of GMOs and keep the state totally GM free. We would request the Prime Minister to reconsider the policy of GM and declare a moratorium at least for the next fifty years.

Chhattisgarh: Before giving permission for commercial cultivation of Bt brinjal, all tests to establish full impacts, including negative impacts, on human and animal health and on the environment should be carried out.

Karnataka: The commercial release of Bt brinjal should be deferred till the issue is thoroughly examined from all the angles by taking into account the views of all stakeholders and conducting a long-term research for its bio-safety and its consequent contributions to food security and farmers' well-being.

Bihar: The Rajya Kisan Ayog is not in favour of the introduction of Bt brinjal in the state at this point of time. The… state government fully endorses the view.

West Bengal: The matter needs thorough examination by the experts in the field.

Orissa: The Government of Orissa does not support the introduction of Bt brinjal at this stage… until sufficient trials are made and interests of small and marginal farmers of the state are safeguarded.

The Minister also informed Parliament about opposition to Bt brinjal from Tamil Nadu, Uttarakhand and Madhya Pradesh.

Secondly, the Minister stated that as far as the objective of reducing pesticide use is concerned, other proven alternatives are available. It is worth recalling that there are now close to 6 lakh farmers in Andhra Pradesh fully practicing NPM (non-pesticide management) agriculture over an area of about 20 lakh acres. I have myself been seeing this initiative over the past four years. The advantage of NPM is that it eliminates chemical pesticide use completely whereas Bt technology only reduces the pesticide spray, albeit substantially. Incidentally, one of the eight missions under the National Action Plan on Climate Change is the National Mission on Sustainable Agriculture of which NPM is an integral part.

Thirdly, the document made it clear said that the tests on the safety of Bt brinjal conducted so far are not adequate.

'While there may be a debate on the nature and number of tests that need to be carried out for establishing human safety, it is incontrovertible that the tests have been carried out by the Bt brinjal developers themselves and not in any independent laboratory. This does raise legitimate doubts on the reliability of the tests, doubts that I cannot ignore.'

Fourthly, the document stated that the contamination threat is very real. 'The fact that brinjal is very largely a cross-pollinated crop according to the generally accepted scientific consensus makes the threat of contamination with the use of Bt brinjal on other varieties a particularly worrisome issue.'

Fifthly, it confirmed that the loss of biodiversity threat is real. Apart from being the world's largest producer of brinjal, India is undoubtedly the country of origin as far as brinjal is concerned... Data made available to me by the National Bureau of Plant Genetic Resources of the ICAR reveals that there are 3,951 collections in the Bureau and the number of diversity-rich districts is 134. The Bureau also points out that diversity-rich regions are likely to be affected by the introduction of Bt brinjal due to gene flow. The loss of diversity argument cannot be glossed over especially when seen in light of the experience we have had in cotton where Bt cotton seed has overtaken non-Bt seeds.

Sixthly, the document refuted the oft stated claim of GM-crop supporters that China is going in rapidly for these crops. Jairam Ramesh said, 'I have spoken with my counterpart in China and he has informed me that China's policy is to encourage research in GM technology but to be extremely cautious when it comes to introduction in food crops.'

In addition, Jairam Ramesh mentioned the negative views on Bt brinjal he received from several eminent scientists.

Professor GE Seralini from France pointed out several flaws in the EC-II report and concludes that 'the risk on human and mammalian health is too high for authorities to take the decision to commercialise this GM brinjal.'

Dr David Schubert of the Salk Institute of Biological Studies, US, says Bt brinjal should not be introduced in India since it poses serious environmental and health risks, will increase social and political dependence on private companies and will entail higher costs at all levels of the food chain.

Jairam Ramesh went on, 'I have had a discussion with both the Director-General of the Indian Council of Medical Research as well as with the Drug Controller to the Government of India. Both have recommended that chronic toxicity and other associated tests should be carried out independently. The parallel has been drawn with drugs where during the crucial clinical trials phase, independent testing is carried out on human beings instead of relying on just the data generated by the developer companies themselves. The DG-ICMR told me that in the face of contradictory evidence of the health effects he would advocate more caution and further tests.'

Doctors for Food and Safety, a network of around 100 doctors across the country, have sent a representation on the health hazards related to GM foods in general and Bt brinjal in particular. They have drawn attention to the recommendations made by the American Academy of Environmental Medicine that GM foods have not been properly tested for human consumption and that there are substantial risks associated with the use of GM foods.

I have also been informed that the Indian Systems of Medicine including ayurveda, siddha, homeopathy and unani use brinjal as a medicinal ingredient, both in raw and cooked form, for treatment of respiratory diseases and that the entire brinjal plant is used in such preparations. There is fear that Bt brinjal will destroy these medicinal properties due to loss of synergy, differences in the alkaloids and changes in other active principles.

Jairam Ramesh has emphasised legal support for an approach based on caution. The Supreme Court has invoked the precautionary principle as a guiding instrument in environmental decisions. There is nothing to prevent decision-makers from assessing the record and concluding there is inadequate information on which to reach determination. If it is not possible to make a decision with 'some' confidence, then it makes sense to err on the side of caution and prevent activities that may cause serious or irreparable harm. An informed decision can be made at a later stage when additional data is available or resources permit further research.

Keeping in view all these factors, Jairam Ramesh chose his words carefully while announcing the moratorium on Bt brinjal.

Based on all the information... and when there is no clear consensus within the scientific community itself, when there is so much opposition from the state governments, when responsible civil society organisations and eminent scientists have raised many serious questions that have not been answered satisfactorily, when the public sentiment is negative and when Bt brinjal will be the very first genetically-modified vegetable to be introduced anywhere in the world and when there is no over-riding urgency to introduce it here, it is my duty to adopt a cautious, precautionary principle-based approach and impose a moratorium on the release of Bt brinjal, till such time independent scientific studies establish, to the satisfaction of both the public and professionals, the safety of the product from the point of view of its long-term impact on human health and environment, including the rich genetic wealth existing in brinjal in our country.

A moratorium implies rejection of this particular case of release for the time being; it does not, in any way, mean conditional acceptance. This should be clearly understood.

There is strong evidence and argument in favour of moratorium on Bt brinjal. If to this we add the vast and growing opinion of eminent scientists on the manifold hazards and uncertainties of GM crops in general, then it is very clear that the moratorium should continue. Vested interests were trying to use Bt brinjal to clear the path for introduction of many other GM food crops as well.

Kuruganti has said that Bt brinjal is a genetically modified food crop created by inserting a bacterial gene from the soil bacterium Bacillus thuringiensis into the brinjal DNA to make the plant produce a toxin against a particular pest (fruit & shoot borer).

This is being sought to be introduced in India, the Philippines and Bangladesh on the claim that it will bring down pesticide use in brinjal/eggplant/aubergine cultivation, reduce pest-related losses and increase yields and bring in better incomes for farmers. While these are the claims around this novel produce, there are many unaddressed concerns around Bt brinjal even as there are also unanswered questions on the very rationale extended for wanting to bring in the Bt food crop.

Bt brinjal was sought to be made into the Trojan horse by the biotech promoters and proponents for an easier entry of various GM seeds and such technologies into India's food and farms sector. This was quite apparent to everyone and the ones who were resisting Bt brinjal were also aware of this.

What the vested interests want is not just Bt brinjal but to open up India's entire food and agriculture system for GM crops. Trials on about 40 such crops have been taking place, including basic staples as rice. Multinational companies want to gain control over India's food and agriculture. They have already cornered the support of some of India's leading politicians and technocrats. One has to prepare for a long struggle to prevent a destruction of India's food and farming system.

3.8 Genetic Engineering and Biological Warfare

Biological warfare is known to be one of the most destructive yet secretive forms of warfare. Its strength derives to a large extent from the fact that it can unleash so much damage without the identity of a specific attack, not to mention the attacker, becoming clear. Biological warfare (also called germ warfare) can be used to spread disease among human beings or destroy crops on a large scale. Protection against such an attack is extremely difficult, especially in the case of a surprise aggression.

According to the Stockholm International Peace Research Institute, the insidious effects of many chemical and biological warfare agents make them suited to sabotage. They not only cause widespread damage but their delayed effects may enable the saboteur to escape detection.

American expert Katheleen C Bailey stated, 'Although biological warfare and toxin warfare were historically viewed as less practical weapons because of technical problems in production and effective delivery, tremendous technology advances such as genetic engineering and development of stabilizers have made these weapons relatively easy to manufacture and deliver effectively. Because these weapons are inexpensive and comparatively easy to produce, an increasing number of nations may pursue them.'

The use of biological and toxin weapons was outlawed by the 1972 Biological and Toxin Weapons Convention. Nevertheless, biological warfare research continued in several countries, especially the US and the USSR. Then Russian President Boris Yeltsin admitted in 1992 that an epidemic of anthrax in Ural mountains in 1979 was caused by an accident at a biological warfare production plant.

The *Third World Guide 1991-92* reported, 'Early in the Reagan administration, a systematic campaign was initiated to develop military capacity based on advances in biomedical and biotechnology such as genetic engineering. These efforts included attempts to undermine the Biological Weapons Convention of 1972, sharply increasing expenditures for biological weapons' research and development, active recruitment of University scientists into Department of Defence and formal testimony before the US Congress in 1986 urging the development of military capacity in biotechnology.'

Senior American journalist William Blum reported, 'In 1956 and 1958, declassified documents revealed that the US Army (released) swarms of specially bred mosquitoes in Georgia and Florida to see whether disease carrying insects could be weapons in a biological war. The mosquitoes bred for the tests were of Aedes Aegypti type, the precise carrier of dengue fever as well as other diseases.' In 1967, it was reported by *Science* magazine that at the US government centre in Fort Detrick, Maryland, dengue fever was amongst those diseases that are at least the object of considerable research and that appear to be among those regarded as potential biological warfare agents.

Cuba protested time and again against the possible involvement of chemical and biological warfare agents in the destruction of its crops, outbreak of African swine and dengue fever. But such is the nature of biological warfare that conclusive evidence is difficult to get.

As biological warfare research was continued by the big powers, one of the main problems they faced was in conducting field tests and other experiments which could prove dangerous for their own people. This problem was solved to some extent by shifting thesc experiments to developing countries in the garb of development and health research.

Disturbing evidence of several such research projects in India was made available in 1975 in the 167th report of Public Accounts Committee of the Indian Parliament titled *Foreign Participation or Collaboration in Research Products in India* and in its follow up report in 1976. These reports indicted a Genetic Control of Mosquitoes Unit (GCMU) project, a microbial pesticide project and some others.

An article published in the *New Scientist* said, 'If one were intending a yellow fever attack on India, this information collected by the GCMU would be very useful.'

Indian news magazine *The Week* alleged in two cover stories (October 9, 1994 and July 23, 1995) that the outbreak of pneumonic plague in Surat in Gujarat was the result of biological warfare experiments conducted by the

US. It said that several suspicious circumstances led it to suspect from the outset that the microbe was not a natural plague bacterium but one mutated in some germ-warfare lab. The magazine said the laboratories which examined the microbe strains collected from Surat have reported that they are different from all known natural strains of the plague germ, Yersinia Pestis. It said that American scientists have been developing a germ detector device known as BIDS (Biological Integrated Detection System). This required field tests some of which, the Week said, may have been conducted in Surat.

Summarizing the reason why suspicions persist, a news report released by the Press Trust of India said, 'While the final report of the Ramalingaswami Committee on Surat plague is yet to be released, there is increasing suspicion among scientists that the strain of Yersinia Pestis, which caused the outbreak, was genetically engineered. Basis for this suspicion is a test report from the US Centre for Disease Control at Fort Collins in Colarado that the Surat strain is unique and not related to any known strain of the plague bacillus.'

Big Business and International Trade

The supermarkets are at present crammed with food, and the productivity of American agriculture is at present enormous. But this is a productivity based on the ruin both of the producers and of the sources of production. City people are not worried about this, apparently, only because they do not know anything about farming. People who know about farming, who know what the farmland requires to remain productive, are worried.

—Wendell Berry
American farmer-philosopher

4.1 Corporatization Has Harmed Farming

The most prominent feature of farming globally in recent decades is growing corporate control. This has often been at the expense and interests of farmers. It is important to understand the wide-ranging adverse implications of this phenomenon for the sustainability of farming systems, welfare of ordinary farmers and food security.

As seeds play the most basic role in agriculture, it is not surprising that corporate interests assigned the greatest importance to strengthening their control over this sector.

Till about 60 to 70 years back, the farming systems of most countries, particularly tropical countries, were characterized by a very rich diversity of seeds and crop varieties, the result of nature's bounty as well as hundreds or thousands of years of careful observation, selection and protection by farmers. They had detailed knowledge about these diverse seeds. This had enabled them to maintain some self-reliance and autonomy despite all the exploitative practices of the earlier colonial system. India alone had thousands of rice varieties.

The first step of the corporate sector was to try to replace the diversity of indigenous seeds with a much narrower genetic base of varieties which will necessarily have to use chemical fertilizers and pesticides to get good yields. This was done in the name of the so-called green revolution. This led to a very rapid erosion of bio-diversity in agriculture.

The harm done to biodiversity of rice, the most important food crop in India, by the new seeds during the early stage of the green revolution was described by an officially constituted task force on rice breeding chaired by Dr RH Richharia in 1979. 'This narrow genetic base has created alarming uniformity, causing vulnerability to diseases and pests. Most of the released varieties are not suitable for typical uplands and low lands which together constitute about 75 percent of the total rice area of the country.'

Thus, experts confirmed that the new varieties being introduced were not suitable to most of our farming area. In addition, they were more susceptible to pests and diseases. Yet this strategy of farming was continued as it led to bigger profits for corporate interests.

Once farmers became dependent on these seeds, the next step for the corporate sector was to expand rapidly in this sector. This process was helped by 'gene robbery', a term used by activists to refer to the trend of developed countries to collect the genetic wealth of bio-diversity of developing countries and use this to obtain and sell their seeds and related inputs to the latter at huge profits.

Pat Roy Mooney, a veteran on this issue who received the prestigious Right to Livelihood Award has written, 'Industrialized governments—often overruling the intentions of their scientists—have come to hoard germplasm and to stock seeds as part of the arsenal of international power diplomacy. Private companies in the North—although glad to receive free genes—are loath to divulge or share the adaptations they draw from these donations.'

The big seed companies expanded in two ways: first, by buying the smaller seed companies at a rapid pace and, secondly, by taking up the production, directly or through related companies, of chemical pesticides and herbicides linked to these seeds.

Another step towards achieving a vice-like grip was to improve the technology of genetic engineering in a big way to spread GM or genetically modified crops. This made it more convenient for bigger companies using more sophisticated technologies to increase their domination. The world seed and agro-chemical industries got heavily concentrated in a few companies. Multi-billion dollar deals were made to boost this concentration.

Similarly, marketing of important crops increasingly got concentrated in the hands of a few multinationals. Some companies directly or indirectly gained ownership of huge monocultures of plantation farming. Others resorted to contract farming on exploitative terms to have assured access to huge quantities of certain crops. Their methods were invariably more chemical input-intensive and capital intensive, causing more environmental ruin but contributing few satisfactory, sustainable jobs.

Yet another device was to introduce a strong and unjust system of patents or somewhat similar intellectual property rights for seed and plant varieties. A new way of imposing this on developing countries was to include intellectual property rights in the new trade regime of the WTO introduced in place of GATT. Even though developing countries tried rather desperately to include some safeguards, the overall impact was to push corporate control to higher levels.

Other aspects of the changing trade regime also led to disruptive impacts on the livelihoods of small farmers of developing countries. Under the new trade regime, these small farmers had to face a lot of unfair competition from imports from developed countries whose farming and marketing systems were dominated by huge agribusiness giants. These cornered a big chunk of the massive farm subsidies paid by their governments to the farm sector.

The power of food and farm MNCs shot up due to the unwavering support they got from their governments. Henry Miller, formerly in charge of biotechnology at the Food and Drug Administration, has written, 'In this area, the US government agencies have done exactly what big agribusiness has asked them to do and told them to do.'

Another trend for big business was to use corruption unabashedly to advance their interests. Dr Pushpa Bhargava, appointed by the Supreme Court to protect safety concerns regarding genetic engineering, opposed the onslaught of multinational companies on farming systems. He warned against the corrupt practices used by them to buy support of governments of developing countries.

He wrote, 'According to the US Securities and Exchange Commission, Monsanto bribed at least 140 Indonesian officials or their families to get Bt cotton approved without environmental impact assessment. In 2005, the firm paid $1.5 million in fine to the US Justice Department for graft. This is one of the many penalties Monsanto has paid in its country of origin in spite of its close ties with the US government and its various regulatory agencies.'

More recently, farmers' organizations have become better aware of the dangers of rapid corporatization of agriculture. This is why they are resisting legislative and other measures of the government which increase corporatization. It is in this wider context that the emerging opposition of farmers to corporatization of farming in several countries, particularly India, should be understood.

4.2 Why MNCs Want to Push GM/GE crops?

Eminent scientists who have examined the technology of genetically engineered (GE) or genetically modified (GM) crops have concluded that it is a highly hazardous and risky technology. Eminent scientists from several countries who make up the Independent Science Panel have said, 'GM crops have failed to deliver the promised benefits and are posing escalating problems on the farm... GM crops should be firmly rejected now.'

Prof Marcello Buiatti (Plant Genetics Department, University of Florence) has summarised the experience of two decades of genetic engineering. 'Plant and animal genetic engineering has developed only two products in more than twenty years - despite the research work of hundreds of thousands of highly skilled technologists and huge financial investments. It can, therefore, be considered the worst failure of the whole history of innovation in agriculture.'

The question is - why are some multinationals so eager to promote such hazardous and risky crops? The answer is that these companies are not interested in improving food security. They are only interested in tightening their grip over the world's food and farming system to earn huge profits. They are not bothered about any adverse impact on farmers, consumers and environment: hunger may worsen, fertile fields may get contaminated and a large number of unsuspecting people and animals may fall seriously ill.

If we look at the trends in world food and agriculture, the domination of the multinational companies is so stark. The way in which patents were incorporated into the WTO agenda and in a very clever way, almost all countries were forced to change their patent laws in keeping with the interests of developed countries. This shows how powerful forces work. The new patent laws helped the food and farming giants to tighten their control on plants and seeds resources of the developing countries.

Genetic erosion of their plant wealth has proved very expensive for farmers, particularly in developing countries. Due to the combined impact of destruction of natural forests and the introduction of green revolution agriculture, genetic erosion has taken place on a massive scale even in countries which were the original source of much of plant diversity. Soon thousands of varieties of plants were lost for eternity. Already several of these had been stored carefully in the labs and gene banks of Europe and North America whose scientists had been engaged in collecting them for several years. Suddenly, in a span of a few decades, the natural advantage which some parts of the world had enjoyed for millions of years appeared to have been reversed. It is unlikely that thc countries from where most of the material came will have free access to them.

Pat Roy Mooney brings out the glaring injustice. It is a raw material unlike any other in the world. It has not been bought. It has been donated. It has been donated by the poor to the rich. The donation has been made under a noble banner proclaiming that genetic resources form a part of the heritage of all humanity and thus can be owned by no one. But as the primary building blocks of agriculture, genes have incalculable political and economic importance. Industrialized governments – often overruling the intentions of their scientists – have come to hoard germplasm and to stock seeds as part of the arsenal of international power diplomacy. Private companies in the North – although glad to receive free genes – are loath to divulge or share the adaptations they draw from these donations.

It was noticed about two decades back that the nature of the seed industry was changing in several countries, particularly in the West (although similar changes also took place in several developing countries). The seed industry had earlier been based on small firms. These were now being gobbled by big companies, especially with major stakes in agri-chemical industry. Within a decade, chemical corporations spent over $10 billion in buying up seeds companies. The American Seed Trade Association even organized a symposium on 'How to sell your seed company.'

Apprehensions were rightly voiced that a small number of giant companies will control seeds as well as agri-chemicals, and that the production of seeds can be given such an orientation as to require high and increasing amounts of agri-chemicals. According to one widely quoted estimate, at least 27 corporations initiated 63 programmes to develop herbicide tolerant crops. Already a few multinational companies control a very considerable part of the international seeds sector and pesticides.

These trends were strengthened further by the developments in the controversial technology of genetic engineering. A very important part of genetic engineering research has been devoted to herbicide-tolerant plant varieties, for example, cotton, which is tolerant to an herbicide called Bromoxynil.

Soon the genetic engineering companies shifted to the even more obnoxious technology of introducing pesticide properties within the plants. About these trends, the Independent Science Panel has said, 'Bt proteins, incorporated into 25 percent of all transgenic crops worldwide, have been found harmful to a range of non-target insects. Some of them are also potent immunogens and allergens. A team of scientists has cautioned against releasing Bt crops for human use.'

Despite this warning, shared by many eminent scientists, the main company involved is willing to go to any length, bribery, coercion, lies, manipulation – to spread its obnoxious technology. Its objective is not food security but to tighten its hold on the food and farming system.

Genetic engineering is important in this quest for dominance as this complex and expensive technology is concentrated to a large extent in the hands of a few multinationals and their subsidiaries. The story that started with snatching the plant resources of tropical/developing/poor countries, led to new patent/IPR laws and finally to genetic engineering. This is the carefully manipulated route these companies, blessed by their governments (particularly in the US), have followed in their race to control the world food system.

This quest is seen perhaps most clearly in the pursuit of what is called the 'Terminator Technology'. A paper published in the *Ecologist* by Ricarda A Steinbrecker and Pat Roy Mooney summarises its implications.

'The Terminator does more than ensure that farmers can't successfully replant their harvested seed. It is the "platform" upon which companies can load their proprietary genetic traits, patented genes for herbicide-tolerance or insect-resistance and get the farmers hooked on their seeds and caught in the chemical treadmill.'

Between 15 and 20 percent of the world's food supply is grown by poor farmers who save their seed. These farmers feed at least 1.4 billion people. The Terminator 'protects' companies by risking the lives of these people. Since Terminator Technology has absolutely zero agronomic benefit, there is no reason to jeopardize the food security of the poor by gambling with genetic engineering in the field. Whether the Terminator works immediately or later, in either instance it is biological warfare on farmers and food security.

It is good that several eminent scientists are coming forward to warn their governments against the potentially disastrous approach of powerful multinational companies.

In a review of trends, *Food Without Choice* (*Tribune*), Bhargava drew pointed attention to the 'attempt by a small but powerful minority to propagate genetically modified (GM) crops to serve their interests and those of multinational corporations, the bureaucracy, the political set-up and a few unprincipled and unethical scientists and technologists'.

He warned, 'The ultimate goal of this attempt in India, of which the leader is Monsanto, is to obtain control over

Indian agriculture and thus food production. With 60 percent of our population engaged in agriculture and living in villages, this would essentially mean not only a control over our food security but also over our farmer security, agricultural security and security of the rural sector.'

As people's consciousness about the hazards of GM crops grew, many US products were refused by its trading partners. This alarmed GM giants and gave them an additional reason to push GM crops in important developing countries so that alternative sources for supply of non-GM products or products not contaminated by GM crops cannot emerge. The US administration and the big GMO (Genetically modified organisms) companies have established such close links that there are unwritten directives from the highest levels not to deny clearance to GMOs on environment, health and related grounds.

Corruption enables MNCs to achieve quick results. A report by US financial risk assessor Innovest stated: It is understandable that the US Government has essentially taken the industry position on GE (Genetic Engineering) safety and labelling.... US Government support for GE crops appears to stem from the fact that the crops are mostly US-developed and the GE companies have made substantial financial contributions to US politicians and political parties. This is not said as a criticism of politicians, but rather of the campaign finance-system, which allows politicians to accept money from the firms they are supposed to regulate. Money flowing from GE companies to politicians as well as the frequency with which GE company employees take jobs with US regulatory agencies (and vice versa) creates large bias potential and reduces the ability of investors to rely on safety claims made by the US Government. It also helps to clarify why the US Government has not taken a precautionary approach to GE and continues to suppress GE labelling in the face of overwhelming public support for it.

In the case of a genetically engineered drug to increase milk production, the FDA approved it despite being in possession of highly damaging information of its adverse impact on animal and human health. In 1990, The House Committee of the US investigated the issue and charged that the concerned company and the FDA 'have chosen to suppress and manipulate animal health test data - in efforts to approve commercial us'.

Despite all this cronyism and corruption, it needs to be noted that in the US GM crops have only been given the status of 'GRAS' or 'Generally recognised as safe' for a long time instead of the stronger, clearer clearance of 'safe for human consumption'.

In India also linkages between officials and GMO companies can be seen in several instances such as the illegal release of GMOs to start with and the way in which estimates of damages suffered by Bt cotton crop were brought down. Unknown to most people and even neighbourhood farmers, several highly unsafe and questionable trials of GM crops were permitted.

Another serious issue of concern relates to the efforts of MNCs to penetrate, influence, corrupt and dominate the national farm research. Seedling is considered one of the world's best journals on seeds and farmers rights.

In the context of the Bt brinjal episode, this journal wrote:

'Indian farmers have good reason to be particularly concerned about this. They have for years in good faith allowed scientists to gather genetic material from their crops and store it in agricultural universities and research institutes. All this cross-institute movement of plant material is making many ask some very fundamental questions: to whom do seed and crop materials really belong? Does the public sector National Agricultural Research System (NARS), entrusted with farmers' varieties, have the power to pass on the material to private corporations? And even if there is acknowledgement of the years of local farming knowledge behind the folk varieties of brinjal by sharing any "benefits", can the loss of pure, natural, genetically untampered - with indigenous varieties be reversed or recompensed? Most of all, can large corporations backed by their governments be allowed to take over farming?'

There was also a series of 'transfers' and 'approvals', which happened with characteristic lack of transparency. First, the National Bureau of Plant Genetic Resources authorized Mahyco to import parental lines from Bangladesh. Then in 2007, the National Biodiversity Authority (NBA), India's main decision-making authority in this field, gave Mahyco clearance to send back the material, now genetically modified, to East West Seeds Bangladesh Ltd for seed distribution. Mahyco has operations in Thailand, Indonesia, Vietnam and the Philippines. In other words, the NBA actually authorised a multinational company to use Indian germplasm to develop a GM product that would not only be used in India but also exported to India's neighbours, endangering Asia's biodiversity.

'Some farmers believe that Mahyco's offer to "provide the technology free of cost" to the NARS is nothing less than a ploy by the GM industry to penetrate the NARS and to leave farmers with little option but to accept Mahyco's products. For all the talk of the benefits of Bt brinjal, farmers clearly see that the introduction of this first GM food crop would start a process that would seriously jeopardise India's food and farm systems and the biodiversity that sustains them. They are determined to struggle against it.' (Reproduced in *Combat Law*, March-April 2010 special issue on Bt brinjal Saga).

In developing countries, large-scale corrupt practices of GMO companies have been documented. In India, there are many tell-tale signs that this corruption has reached up to very high levels, including some Ministers known to be ruthless. So, learning from Mahatma Gandhi, one should prepare for a nationwide satyagraha to save our country from danger of GM/GE crops.

On one hand, many eminent scientists are rejecting GM crops. Their view is supported by the adverse reports from farmers. On the other hand, the GE companies have invested billions of dollars to literally take over the world food and farming system. To do so, they have to make serious hazards acceptable. They are spending huge amounts to make their blatant lies appear as scientific truth. Their campaign is particularly strong in countries like India because they want to destroy the capability of leading farming countries to supply GMO-free food to the world market.

So, the stakes are very high for the multinationals. But they are even higher for Indian people and farmers whose very survival is threatened by GM crops.

4.3 Ulterior Agenda for Food and Farming

The dangers of increasing corporatization of farming and food sectors has been much discussed in India. This is welcome because there needs to be increasing public awareness of this harmful and high-risk trend.

In the course of this discussion, the names of two billionaires have been increasingly taken. This is understandable as their business houses are regarded as the most favoured in the entrenched crony capitalism. But this has also led to a certain oversimplification of the discourse. This distracts attention from a much wider and in fact more powerful range of forces that threatens to badly disrupt the food and farming system of India and many other countries.

What are these powerful forces and what are their aims and strategies? It is very important to understand this if a credible resistance is to be organized in time to protect food security, food sovereignty, agro-ecology and the sustainable livelihoods of rural communities.

At the core of this highly selfish and disruptive effort are a number of giant multinationals, having local subsidiaries and branches in many countries. They are not just competing with each other but also having surprising levels of collaborative actions to promote common and joint interests. One way of concentrating power is by mergers. These allow companies which acquire too much disrepute from unethical activities to hide their previous identity and find a new one. While earning obnoxious profits from food and farming is a more commonly understood aim of these corporations, an even more prized but less discussed aim is to gain more and more dominance over the food and farming sector. For this, increasing concentration, particularly in the seeds sector, is emphasized; within the seeds sector their focus is mostly on GM seeds, which facilitates dominance, as well as patenting and linking of particularly specified agro-chemicals to their seeds. The ultimate aim of these corporations is to concentrate control of food/farming sector from seeds to farming to processing to dining table in a few hands.

These giant companies do not just promote their interests on their own. They obtain more influential help of the regimes in various countries, setting aside huge funds for legally permissible lobbying and political donations as well as corrupt practices. The success of these efforts is evident from the fact that in many countries these companies can count on the collaboration of senior officials, scientists and politicians.

Thirdly, these companies have the explicit or implicit backing of several leading international organizations which promote mainly big business. Some of them present themselves as philanthropic organizations. They have acquired special skills in giving big business interests the cover of sustainability and public good. Some have targeted the critical food/farming and health sectors in particular.

Fourthly, there is an increasing effort by these business interests to infiltrate and/or co-opt the United Nations system, agencies and officials so that their agenda gets much more credibility. An additional advantage is that many experts and consultants working with the UN get collaborators within governments. Of course, some honest persons within the UN system resist this.

In addition, big businesses have a massive hold over the media as providers of huge advertisement revenue as well as other benefits. Not all media outlets accept these benefits.

Last but not the least, the big companies try to win over many NGOs, including those working at grassroots, by giving them projects. They also fund some farmer organizations, directly or indirectly, to compromise them or buy their support. Several honest persons within the NGO sector resist this strongly.

4.4 Global Corporate Control

Amid increasing questions about corporatization in India, corporate control over farming and farmers (small and medium farmers as well as family farms) is being questioned almost all over the world including the US. Bedabrat Pain, an ex-NASA scientist toured the US countryside with three colleagues to understand the reality of corporate control and the resulting problems of farmers. The quotes below are from his report, *How Big Ag Ate Up America's Small Farms*:

'Nearly all the farmers we talked to hold the Reagan-era 'opening up' of agriculture and the rise of 'Big Ag' – gigantic agro-business that now dominate American farming – responsible for their plight… Shorn of government support a quarter million small farmers closed, over a million generational farmers were displaced, and deserted towns began dotting the rural landscape. What happened to the land? Unsurprisingly Big Ag gobbled it up as landless farmers started toiling under onerous contract farming terms. Giant corporations used financial clout to control the market, depress farm-gate prices, buy infrastructure for a song, and raise costs to a point where small farms became unsustainable.'

This account would no doubt shock many people who have generally a benevolent and picturesque view of American farming. But the US is not at all alone in experiencing large-scale displacement and distress. In Mexico, nearly a million farmers were displaced in the aftermath of the introduction of trade treaty called NAFTA which brought cheap subsidized imports from the US against which Mexican farmers could not compete.

In India, a comparison of 2001 and 2011 census data reveals a reduction of 8.6 million farmers and even a bigger rise in the number of rural landless households.

The harmful legal changes made in the Reagan-era bears comparison with the debate now in India regarding the impact of the three new farm laws against which farmers were protesting.

What happens is that when there is a lot of opposition to some adverse changes like laws, the long term problems tend to be forgotten or neglected. While criticising the Reagan-era changes, the corporatization trends of earlier years which too were problematic get overlooked. Again, the intense debate on the farm laws in India has led to the neglect of several disturbing trends from earlier times.

The US experiences reveal the extent to which corporate control has proceeded. A handful of meat processing companies now own the livestock while poultry, beef and pig farmers are more or less serfs—raising the animals for them under contract. They have no bargaining power because these food giants are the only players left in town. Nearly 75 percent of all US poultry farmers today live below the poverty line while Big Ag control everything from 'farm to fork' and from seeds to grocery stores. Four large firms control at least two-thirds of the seed market, 80 percent of chemical fertilizers, grain trading, dairy production, meat supply and almost 100 percent of farm machinery. Meanwhile, government money flows to the corporations in the form of write-offs, market facilitations and crop insurance subsidies. Over 70 percent of the $50 billion in US government subsidies goes to the top 20 percent of farms. John E Ikerd, retired Professor Emeritus at University of Missouri, says this couldn't have happened without political patronage.

This is a very disturbing picture which shows that domination of a few big corporations is accompanied by increasing marginalization and disempowerment of farmers till they are reduced to virtual serfs in contract farming or under somewhat similar legal arrangements. This disturbing and harmful trend is manipulated in such a way that the big business interests continue to get the most financial benefits from government spending on agriculture.

The wider reality is that despite these injustices of the West, there are likely to be social security arrangements to protect the most marginalized sections from the worst impacts of poverty. But such protection is likely to be denied to the marginalized or displaced sections in poorer or less prosperous countries including India.

Hence, one of the most urgent but neglected issues is not just increasing agricultural production but doing it on sustainable and protected farms of small and medium farmers. This is an important justice issue. It should be highlighted that small and medium farmers alone are able to provide the care of soil and land and animals and water sources which is so essential for sustainability. This cannot be provided by big business farming with all its heavy machines and truckloads of agro-chemicals.

4.5 Unfair Trade and Hunger

In most discussions on food and farming systems in India, fears are raised that pressures and interpretations of the World Trade Organization (WTO) rules can cause problems for farmers and the public distribution system (PDS) for food. A large number of India's mostly small farmers face many serious problems due to a variety of factors.

These concerns exist not just for India but for several developing countries. The overwhelming majority of farmers are small farmers, who have a very low resource base. Their risk bearing capacity is limited. If they face a sudden price crash due to cheap imports, they will find it very difficult to recover from these losses. If this is repeated for some time, their precarious but proud existence as small farmers may be threatened. They will be forced to sell their land to recover from debts or feel that they can no longer bear further high risk.

The Human Development Report (HDR) prepared a special issue on international trade which focused attention to some aspects of the threat posed by unfair trade to small peasants in developing countries. The HDR questions the globalisation hype by drawing attention to those who have suffered. It said, 'Participation in trade can exacerbate inequality as poor people absorb the adjustment costs of increased competition from imports, while people with assets and market power take advantage of opportunities provided by exports.'

For example, increased exports of high value added fruit and vegetables from countries like Kenya and Zambia have been concentrated in large capital-intensive farms with weak links to the rest of the economy. Similarly, in Brazil, just four or fewer firms account for more than 40 percent of exports of soy, orange juice, poultry and beef while ten million small and landless peasants live below the poverty line in villages.

In 1990s, almost three-quarters (about 75 percent of Kenya's high value-added horticulture exports were supplied by small farmers. By 2000 this share had fallen to 18 percent According to HDR, 'The biggest change to the industry has been the increased importance of farms owned or leased by major export companies.'

What the HDR report does not say is that even if small landholders are integrated into this export trade, this can still lead to longer-term loss if the concentration on export crops is damaging for soil, water and other aspects of environment. When the export demand is curtailed and cash dries up, these small farmers may not be able to go back to their staple food crops.

HDR indicts particularly those unfair trade practices which undermine the livelihoods of small and landless peasants. These practices are linked particularly to the subsidies given by governments of developed countries. HDR says, 'The problem at the heart of the Doha Round negotiations can be summarised in three words-rich country subsidies.... Rich countries spend just over $1 billion a year as aid to developing country agriculture and just under $1 billion a day supporting their own agricultural systems.'

These heavy subsidies hurt rural communities in developing countries. 'Subsidized exports undercut them in global and local markets, driving down the proceeds received by farmers and the wages received by agricultural labourers. Meanwhile producers seeking access to industrial country markets have to scale some of the highest tariff peaks in world trade.'

Within the rich countries, most benefits of farm subsidies go to those who deserve these the least. 'The winners in the annual cycle of billion dollar subsidies are large-scale farmers, corporate agribusiness interests and landowners.' Research carried by HDR showed that subsidy's distribution in rich countries is more unequal than income distribution in Brazil.

So HDR concludes, 'It would be hard to design a more regressive - or less efficient – system of financial transfers than currently provided through agricultural subsidies .... Industrial countries are locked into a system that wastes money at home and destroys livelihoods.'

This has contributed significantly to highly unfair trade. HDR says, 'When it comes to world agricultural trade, market success is determined not by comparative advantage but by comparative access to subsidies – an area in which producers in poor countries are unable to compete.'

In the European Union, farmers and processors are paid four times the world market price for sugar, generating a 4 million tonnes surplus, which is marketed with the help of more than $1 billion in export subsidies (paid to a small group of sugar processors). Subsidised EU sugar exports lower world prices by about one-third, inflicting heavy losses on sugar exporters among developing countries as well as on sugar crop farmers based in developing countries.

At the time the HDR report on trade was prepared, 20,000 cotton farmers in the US were likely to receive government payments of $4.7 billion in a year – an amount equivalent to the market value of the crop. These subsidies lowered world prices by 9-13 percent and enabled US producers to dominate world markets. In Benin the fall in cotton prices in one year was linked to an increase in poverty from 37 percent to 59 percent. Around the same time, rice grown in the US at a cost of $415 a tonne was exported at $274 a tonne. This was made possible by US government payments of $1.3 billion, almost three quarters of the value of output. In countries like Ghana and Haiti, rice farmers were pushed out of national markets by US imports.

According to a widely quoted study by Oxfam

International, the practice of exporting agricultural surpluses on the world market at less than the cost of production – or 'dumping' – is one of the most pernicious aspects of industrialised country trade policies, which the WTO has failed adequately to address. Unfair competition from dumped agricultural produce creates problems for developing countries by depriving them of foreign-exchange earnings and market share, and undermining local production, rural livelihoods, and food security.

This study, titled *Rigged Rules and Double Standards - Trade, Globalisation and the Fight Against Poverty* adds, 'Oxfam has developed a new measure of the scale of export dumping by the EU and the United States. It suggests that both these agricultural superpowers are exporting at prices more than one-third lower than the costs of production. These subsidized exports from rich countries are driving down prices for exports from developing countries and devastating the prospects for small-holder agriculture. In countries such as Haiti, Mexico and Jamaica, heavily subsidised imports of cheap food are destroying local markets. Some of the world's poorest farmers are competing against its richest treasures.'

Concerns of poor countries and poor people have been ignored to an alarming extent at the WTO. According to HDR, 'the agreement on agriculture left most EU and US farm subsidy programmes intact for the simple reason that it was in all but name a bilateral agreement between the two parties that were forced onto the multilateral rules system. In effect, the world's economic superpowers were able to tailor the rules to suit their national policies.'

Perhaps the most disturbing aspect of the emerging international trade regime is that the US and some other developed countries have arranged the classification of subsidies in such a way that very massive subsidies given to their biggest agribusiness companies—which include some of the most powerful and resourceful multinational companies—can be defended as acceptable under WTO rules. But the much more modest subsidies given by developing countries to their small farmers are criticized as violation of WTO rules. This allows the rich countries to strengthen big agribusiness companies domestically by allowing them to gobble up businesses and even the land of smaller farmers. On the other hand, the big companies get more space and power to unleash havoc in developing countries through their highly subsidized products. In addition, several free trade, multilateral and bilateral agreements have greatly increased the problems of small farmers in developing countries. These trends are blatantly unjust. International efforts as well as growing unity of developing countries are urgently needed to check them to create an alternative system of fair and just international trade.

4.6 Free Trade Agreements may Further Aggravate Injustice in International Trade

At the time of the formation of the World Trade Organisation (WTO) and the related international agreements such as Trade-related Intellectual Property Rights (TRIPS), serious apprehensions had been expressed about the adverse impacts on people's livelihoods, health and food security. These apprehensions have by and large turned about to be correct as is evident from the crisis situations faced in several aspects of agriculture (and related activities) as well as industry. In addition the adverse impact of TRIPS on the availability of reasonably priced essential medicines as well as the seeds rights of farmers has been noted. The broad-ranging adverse impacts of the wider reach and deeper penetration of multinational companies and banks in the form of the plunder of natural resources and greater vulnerability of economy are also clear.

While there is a growing need for a proper assessment of all the adverse impacts of the WTO regime and renegotiations based on such an assessment, there is instead a contrary trend of going in for more and more bilateral Free Trade Agreements (FTAs) without even first properly assessing and stabilising the impacts of the earlier changes in foreign trade.

Whereas international trade agreements despite all their inequities, at least have the principle of differential treatment for developing countries, FTAs are much less likely to recognise this. Any agreement between a developing and a developed country can therefore be even more unequal. This possibility increases all the more because in some important respects like tariff reduction and TRIPS some FTAs have shown the tendency to adopt WTO-plus measures. In other words, some important provisions of these agreements may be even more sweeping compared to what has been agreed to in the WTO regime.

In the case of imports, FTAs are likely to offer much steeper and broader reduction of tariffs. Hence the chances of cheaper imports harming the livelihoods of farmers can be higher. This is particularly true in the case of farm imports from those developed countries where heavy farm subsidies are available. Cheap dairy imports, for example, can have a very adverse impact on small scale dairy farmers of developing countries. Income from sale of milk is an important source of subsistence for many poor families.

Similarly, cheap imports can threaten the survival of many micro, small and medium industries, including food-processing industries.

As a result of the implementation of TRIPS-plus proposals the price of essential medicines can rise steeply and thc availability of cheaper generic medicines can decline significantly. The seed rights of farmers can be significantly affected while the grip of multinational companies on agriculture can increase. The share of foreign companies in government purchases can increase and any obstacles in the path of rapid spread of multinational companies are likely to be dismantled. One of the impacts of FTAs is likely to be that large-scale onslaughts on natural resource base are likely to get more approvals.

Earlier, there was a lot of concern regarding the adverse impacts of a free trade agreement with the European Union. There were prolonged negotiations but finally a deal could not be clinched, one of the reasons being widespread concerns about the adverse impacts of a free trade agreement on farming, dairying and related activities in India.

However, now there are greater chances of a free trade agreement being reached with the US, perhaps in phases, which may have even more adverse impact given the more aggressive pursuit of their narrow high profit and domination interests by leading US agro-business companies. In particular, there is concern regarding the adverse impact on domestic production of dairy and poultry products, and several farm products particularly soybeans and maize.

Another adverse impact may be the increasing pressure on India to be more accommodative to the interests of these multinational companies, to the extent of changing laws to accept GM food imports from the US. Ultimately, pressures may extend to getting approval for GM food crops in India, which is likely to be very, very harmful and will also be opposed strongly.

Do Not Forget The Landless Peasant

It is important to stress here that yields per hectare are as high on small as on large farms or under traditional agriculture even higher. With a few notable exceptions, total output per hectare is higher on small farms, chiefly because their intensity of land use is higher. A more equal distribution of production inputs, including services, can only help to strengthen the role of the small farm in expanding production. The fact that some attempts at radical redistribution of land have led initially to lower production does not invalidate the conclusion that after some years a more even distribution of farming resources and inputs should help rather than hinder growth of output.

—**Agriculture towards 2000**

Food and Agriculture Organization (FAO) Report

5.1 Landless in Villages: The Most Vulnerable

Mahatma Gandhi said once the true measure of any society can be found in how it treats its most vulnerable people. What is the most numerous segment of Indian society? The answer:

According to the 2011 census data, a total of 263 million persons (26.3 crore) are involved in farming activities. Out of this, only 119 million are land-owning farmers while 144 million are landless workers and peasants. However, the latter is almost entirely absent in the policy and policy debates on farming.

The increase in this segment of our population has been very rapid in recent times. In the 2001 census, only 107 million landless farm workers were counted. This means that within a decade their number shot up by 37 million (from 107 to 144 million). Only a small part of this could be due to family divisions and population increase. It is clear that a large number of small farmers (and to a lesser extent rural artisan) households have moved towards landless farm worker status. This trend is still continuing as small farmers and rural artisans face growing livelihood problems.

At the same time, the numbers getting counted as landless farm workers can hardly get enough employment in farm work in and around their own villages. One reason is decreased employment generation in farming due to the use of more machinery and weedicides. Secondly, higher levels of alienation of landless Dalits from local elites prevents them from seeking work in their own villages.

Hence, those described frequently as landless farm workers not only do farm work in their own villages (if and when available) but seek work in nearby mines, quarries, construction and industrial work sites, often leaving early morning and returning at night. Many perhaps try to earn income as migrant labourers, working in distant farms, mines, brick-kilns and construction sites, leaving for long seasons of work and returning home for short periods.

In the absence of any caring response from most governments, they have evolved their own coping mechanisms. All this got disrupted due to Covid-19.

As the number of rural landless has zoomed, the only significant national-level response in the last two decades has come in the form of MGNREGA (Mahatma Gandhi National Rural Employment Guarantee Act). While the UPA government deserves credit for enacting this legislation the actual allocations made for the scheme were not adequate.

Once the NDA took over, initially the scheme was criticized at the highest level in the government. However, better sense prevailed and the scheme was retained while denying it adequate budget. The budget was increased to some significant extent only under the Covid special package. By then the need of workers returning home to their states in vast numbers due to a national lockdown had increased so much that even this proved inadequate in checking rural distress, particularly among the landless.

The guarantee component was weakened at the last stages of passing the law. The original guarantee was that if the government cannot provide employment as stated in the legislation, it will give compensatory payment to those who demanded work. This was diluted by adding that this will be subject to government finances. This in practice led to a situation in which this compensatory payment is not made in over 95 percent of the cases.

While the scheme has been monitored more in terms of budget allocation and expenditure as seen in official records, its corruption-ridden implementation has further limited benefits to the landless. So much so that many have lost faith in this. At the same time, where this has been implemented well, it has given a lot of hope. So, the scheme should stay and there should be a widespread campaign for strengthening and expanding it.

However, this scheme by itself cannot provide an adequate and reliable base for the livelihoods of the highly vulnerable rural landless households. For this, two additional measures are needed.

The first is based on the concept of a minimum land holding for all rural households. This may be only a small holding but if supported by water and moisture conservation/minor irrigation and cultivated intensively, using agro-ecology, this can provide a reliable base of food security, good health and firm bonds with the village.

It is often stated that land is just not available for distribution among the poor. But we see that vast tracts of land are always available for corporates. The government machinery helps in facilitating this. Again, a lot of village land is passing into the hands of the urban rich people and moneylenders. It seems that in the present balance of power in India, rural land is available for all except those who need this the most (rural landless workers)!

Finally, small farmers should be helped in ways that

the process of land-alienation is checked. During 2001-11, the number of land-owning farmers decreased from 127 million to 118 million. In other words, within a decade, the number of farmers fell by 8.6 million or reduced by about 2,300 per day. Most of this land passed from the poor to the rich.

When I visited a village in Vidarbha some time back, I was surrounded by land-selling middlemen who were full of offers to sell land. Potential buyers were visiting from urban areas so regularly that I was mistaken to be one!

I learnt in the village that many impoverished and indebted peasants were forced to sell their land. The rich, including politicians, were the main buyers.

So small farmers have to be strengthened to check land alienation. The government should extend a strong helping hand to boost water conservation and minor irrigation in a big way while supporting agro-ecology in important ways. The government should procure healthy food produced by agro-ecology by providing a fair and encouraging price to farmers. Their already accumulated debts can be phased out with government help.

This two-sided approach of helping the rural landless to become small farmers while helping small farmers to avoid land alienation will greatly help to reduce rural poverty and resolve the farming crisis of India.

5.2 India needs more sustainable farming

With growing discontent among farmers and the strengthening of their protest movements in India, it is evident that small and medium farmers, who constitute the overwhelming majority need a more sustainable and just farming system. The government should play an important protective role.

The difficulties a large number of farmers face is evident from the telling figure that nearly 100 small farmers are turned into landless farmers every hour in India. If it takes 15 minutes to read and reflect on this, 25 farmers would have lost their land during this period. This is not a sustainable situation for any farming system based on small farmers.

Before we proceed further, consider these telling statistics. There were 127.3 million (1,273 lakh) land-owning farmers in 2001 and their number reduced to 118.7 million (1,187 lakh) in 2011. In other words, within 10 years, the number had dropped by 8.6 million (86 lakh). This is a huge fall.

There is an even bigger increase in indicating that millions of farmers and to some extent artisans moved to this category. As the reduced number of farmers is more than accounted for in the increase of landless farm workers, we can reasonably assume that nearly 8.6 million farmers moved from the category of farmers to landless farm (or other) workers in a decade. This means a loss of 0.86 million (8.6 lakh) owner farmers in one year or around 72,000 in one month or 2,400 in one day. This implies nearly 100 owner farmers moving into the category of landless farm workers every hour.

Some people claim that this trend towards reduced number of farmers is largely due to sub-division and fragmentation of land. But this is likely to result in marginalization rather than complete loss of land. The pressures resulting from increasing costs and expenses (in turn related to wrong policies in many cases) are likely to constitute a more important factor.

Adverse weather conditions and worsening disasters as well as lack of adequate protection against this (including failure and mismanagement of corruption-ridden insurance schemes) is another important factor.

The inability of a large number of small farmers to get a fair price for their produce plays a major role leading to misery. The minimum support price-based system of government procurement reaches only a small number of farmers at the national level, and that too largely only for wheat and rice.

Due to indiscriminate use of chemical fertilizers and pesticides, the natural fertility of land based largely on organic content of soil has declined. Fertility enhancing mixed farming systems have been replaced by harmful monocultures. Farmer-friendly, fertility boosting earthworms and micro-organisms which increase soil fertility by natural processes have suffered genocidal harm, pollinators like bees and butterflies have declined greatly while water sources are depleted and polluted badly.

All these contribute greatly to the difficulties of farmers and make them try desperate remedies which greatly increase expenses but do not give desirable results as long as the real problems remain. This is deeply worrying because with the accentuation of climate change, some of these issues are likely to accentuate greatly.

The increasing domination of business interests is worsening the already distressing situation. Multinational companies are pushing GM crops with increasing obstinacy despite the mounting evidence of many-sided serious problems and risks associated with them.

At the same time, big business interests are clamouring for a role in dictating crop choice via contract farming and a much bigger role in marketing, stocking and hoarding. With the government increasingly friendly to big business interests, the cause of sustainable farming and interests of small farmers is hit.

It is in this situation that distress and discontent among small and medium farmers has escalated. Hence, there is an urgency to move towards policies which are more protective of sustainable farming and bring justice to landless farm workers, sharecroppers, tenants and small traders.

So, on one hand, we need to support the farmers demanding repeal of the three controversial farm laws to check further domination of the food and farming system by big business, on the other hand, we need to create a more sustainable and protective system for small farmers based on an improved system of government procurement (which reaches out to more small and medium farmers and extends to more crops like oilseeds, pulses and millets) as well a system of social agro-ecology. A revival of the agenda of land reforms as well as better assurance of fair wages and improvements in the rural employment guarantee scheme will help landless farm workers.

5.3 Land Reforms in India

How realistic can be any promise if the most effective means of achieving it is discarded deliberately? If the promises of reducing rural poverty is real, how is that the most promising means of land reforms has been given up before achieving any significant success?

Land reforms have been widely regarded all over the world as an important source of reducing rural inequalities. While their importance was well recognized in the early years of independent India, land reforms were more or less given up before these could make a meaningful contribution to reducing poverty in villages. Now the agenda of redistributing land among the landless has been given up entirely. When it comes to finding land for the landless, it is claimed land is just not available. But land does come up in plenty when it is meant for big corporates.

Despite this highly discouraging attitude of government policy, it is important to re-emphasize the importance of land reforms not just for reducing poverty but also for widening the base to increase farm productivity. While discussing future food and farming trends, the Food and Agriculture Organization (FAO) emphasized that more equal land distribution is likely to increase productivity. 'With a few notable exceptions, total output per hectare is higher on small farms, chiefly because their intensity of land use is higher.' The FAO said the contribution of land reforms to reducing poverty is even more significant. 'Redistribution of only 5 percent of farmland in India, coupled with improved access to water, could reduce rural poverty levels by 30 percent … so that in Indian conditions land and water reform would be a key approach.'

This view is supported by a six-country study by the International Labour Organization (ILO) which estimated that 'if land were equally distributed among all agricultural families (including the landless), and the new equal holdings achieved yields equal to present holdings of the same size and used a similar level of inputs, food output could potentially rise by anything from 10 percent (Pakistan) and 28 percent (Colombia and a rice-growing Malaysian region) to 80 percent in northeastern Brazil.'

India's Planning Commission expressed agreement with the key role of land reforms. 'In an economy where over 60 percent of the population is dependent on agriculture, the structure of land ownership is central to the well-being of the people.' Despite this, the Planning Commission noted a decline in the commitment to land reforms. 'Land reforms seem to have been relegated to the background in the mid-1990s. More recently, initiatives of state governments have related to liberalising of land laws in order to promote large-scale corporate farming.'

A report of the Working Group on Land Relations for Formulation of the Eleventh Five Year Plan was frank. 'There are serious concerns that the phase of economic liberalization may be accompanied by further erosion of land reforms.' Pushpendra, a researcher with the Lal Bahadur Shastri (IAS) Academy, expressed regret that the pro-liberalization lobby is for the removal of all restrictions on leasing, upward revision of ceilings on holdings, concessions to the industry for investing in rural infrastructure, unrestricted entry in rural areas for national and multinational companies, agro-farm houses, food and fruit processing industries to lease-in or purchase land through direct interaction with the peasants, speeding-up the acquisition process by the government, export-led and demand-driven agriculture, and for the removal of all restrictions on conversion of land from farm to non-farm activities. There is also immense pressure on the government to make available land to private parties either through land acquisition process or from its own pool of land meant for distribution to the landless and the small and marginal farmers.

Once the neo-liberal agenda got entrenched in India in the 1990s, for all practical purposes the programme of land reforms was in the process of being jettisoned. This happened without any significant redistribution being achieved in favour of the poor. Former Rural Development Secretary SR Sankaran, known for his candid views, wrote that the extent of land redistributed was 43 percent of agricultural land in China, 37 percent in Taiwan, 32 percent in South Korea and 33 percent in Japan. In India, the efforts of the central and state governments to enact, revise and implement the ceiling laws, spread over 35 years, resulted in the redistribution of only 1.25 percent of the operational area.

Although in public pronouncements the government placed special emphasis on preventing land alienation of tribal communities, here too the reality differed from rhetoric. A review by another senior official, Sukumar Das, stated, 'Land legislation to protect the tribal people has failed to achieve its basic objective. In fact, more than 50 percent of the total land allotted by the government has already been alienated.' What is more, the land acquisition for various projects over the years resulted in tribal communities becoming the biggest losers of their land.

Despite this, there was some new hope in 2005-2008 when the Scheduled Tribes and Traditional Forest Dwellers Forest Rights Act (briefly called Forest Rights Act or simply FRA) was passed and its rules framed. This Act hoped to correct the 'historical injustice' caused to tribal and other forest-dwelling communities.

But this too was belied to a great extent due to several factors. Firstly, the number of rejection of claims was very high. Those whose claim was rejected were often not even informed about it. Secondly, a significant number of deserving households were simply left out as they could not send their claims properly in time. Even when the claims were accepted, the acceptance was only for a small part of land being cultivated earlier.

It is clear that despite all the lip sympathy to cut rural poverty, the programme of greatest potential for this was given up before any real success was achieved. However, it remains extremely important to keep land reforms on the agenda of rural development and change. It has been seen time and again that even small plots of land provided to landless households for growing food or used as kitchen gardens can contribute significantly to improving nutrition and food security.

Where land needs to be under tree cover for ecological reasons, this can be done by giving legal rights to the landless while the land is planted with mixed species of indigenous trees using their wage labour. When trees grow, those who were earlier paid by the government to plant trees can get rights over minor forest produce harvested on sustainable basis. Elsewhere, wage labour or even work under MNREGA can be used to fence degraded land. When there is regeneration of forests, the landless can get minor forest produce rights.

Even modest schemes have a lot of potential of combining ecological regeneration with more land and livelihood rights for the poorest. Bigger redistribution efforts can bring greater benefits. This also gives landless people more stability in the overall rural structure.

5.4 How and Why Farmers Lose Land

In many countries with varying levels of development, a large number of farmers have been losing their land, sometimes even losing their status as independent landowning farmers. Various economic, technological, social, political, legal and other factors are involved. One must not generalize or oversimplify a complex situation. This much can be stated without fear of contradiction that economic and technological factors pushed by big business are often responsible for small and medium farmers losing their land.

In India, a major role is that of who manipulate government policy to suit their interests and impose technologies and systems which are most likely to increase costs, risks, debts and dependence of farmers, pushing them to part with their land.

This is of course never stated in any policy document that farmers have to give up their land. Yet, the most likely impact of what is pushed by big business and other vested interests is that a large number of farmers end up losing their land due to debts and other pressures.

This should be kept in mind while discussing the controversies relating to the three farm laws in India recently. These laws together prepared the ground for a big increase of big business grip on farming and food system of India. The government has stated, rightly, that there is no specific clause in these laws which advocates taking over the land of any farmer. It is even clarified that takeover of a farmer's land is not intended in the new law, including in contract farming. However, protesting farmers insisted that their land is threatened.

These fears need to be understood in the context of the wider threats that increased dominance of business interests on farming and food systems bring. These generate pressures which create conditions, over time, for farmers losing their land. The farmers say that the factors which led to the loss of land by 8.6 million farmers within 10 years would have strengthened with the three farm laws. This understanding is not possible in a clause-to-clause reading of the three laws. Therefore, a comprehensive wider understanding of such issues is needed.

5.5 Women Farmers and Land

Rukha lives in Baraicha village in Banda district of Uttar Pradesh. One day in November 2019 when she went to cultivate her field she was surrounded by several men some of whom attacked her. She was injured badly and her clothes were partially torn. A few hours later when I asked her about her ordeal, she broke down. She kept pointing to her injuries.

Rukha is one of the many women farmers who are victims of attempts by powerful persons to grab their land. Although after the news about her appeared in newspapers and some social activists came to her help, and her problems now appear to be sorted out, her ordeal should be told because it is representative of the tendency of the powerful persons to identify weak women farmers and try to grab their land.

Rukha is a very weak and fragile woman bringing up two small children. Her problems started when a dominant man in the village who had constructed a house near her land started trying to grab her family fields, the only source of their livelihood. Her husband is a simple man. The land grabbers first attacked him in June in his field. Rukha rushed to his rescue and with folded hands requested the tormentors to stop beating him. They thrashed her as well with sticks and even tried to disrobe her. This was an attempt to humiliate and scare her as she is known to resist injustice.

Rukha took the entire family to the police station. The police were initially sympathetic but then mysteriously they started threatening the family instead of taking any action against the attackers.

Her husband was harassed by land grabbers to such an extent that one day he simply went away to some unknown destination. Now Rukha's problems became almost unbearable. She had to bring up her children while working alone for livelihood and facing constant harassment and threats.

At this stage someone introduced her to a women's organization, Chingari, which intervened with the police and officials on her behalf. This gave new hope to Rukha.

She again started to cultivate her field. Just when things seemed to be settling down came a new assault on November 2, indicating that the land grabbers were probably fixing up some higher connections before going on the offensive.

The next day the police were initially reluctant to lodge a report or to get a medical examination done. It was only when Chingari activists persisted that the police took halting steps.

This is not the story of Rukha alone. In Sulkhan Ka Purwa village in the same region (Naraini Block), Kammo was building a house on her own land. Her husband had migrated to Mumbai some time back. Seeing her alone, a local man said she will have to pay Rs 20,000 before erecting her house. When she refused, she was beaten mercilessly by goons as well as policemen. Her wounds did not heal for a long time.

In several villages of Bundelkhand and other areas where male migration among weaker sections is high, their women are harassed, humiliated and beaten by dominant persons and thugs. The motive generally is to grab some or all of their land or plunder their meager resources.

One device used is to get land records altered using their muscle and money power. They also bribe the policemen.

Says a leading activist of Chingari, 'We have seen several such cases in recent times when women faced violence due to a wider conspiracy to grab their land. When a husband is absent and the conspirators know he is unlikely to return for some time, the woman becomes more vulnerable.'

About her experiences, she says, 'I was really shocked at the kind of extreme violence inflicted on Rukha and

Kammo. Despite this they did not get immediate help on their own. It is only after our intervention that some initial steps were taken.'

In times of increasing migration of male members from millions of households in villages, particular attention should be given to protecting women farmers and workers. It must be ensured that their farm or housing land is not grabbed and encroached upon. Widows who try to cultivate their fields are harassed in various ways, sometimes even by relatives, in a bid to grab their land. All single women are very vulnerable.

5.6 Many-sided Rural Crisis

An important strength of India is that about two-thirds of its people live in villages. As the world grapples with life-endangering environmental problems, the rural base of a country can be an important source of resilience in protecting life-nurturing conditions and getting close to self-reliance in terms of meeting basic needs. However, in the absence of proper priorities and policies, multiple crises have emerged in our villages, including the economic crisis of farmers. Here we discuss the problems of 12 groups in rural India, each one of which is important in its own way. Most of the crises have multiplied in Covid times.

Firstly, most landless farm households take up casual farm and non-farm work in and around villages. Some still have more regular arrangements with a single, relatively bigger, landowner. The number of these households is likely to be more than owner cultivator households. The farm work opportunities have decreased greatly due to mechanization. These households have very low resource base. They have very low food-stocks and savings to fall back upon in difficult times. Work opportunities in non-farm employment have declined steeply in Covid times. These households are often the poorest in any village.

Secondly, there are migrant workers who are generally among the poorest. But in several cases they have managed to temporarily improve their income from migrant work. Their coping mechanism broke badly after the pandemic, leading to acute distress. Another aspect of these households is that often only small children and/or elderly persons are left behind. Life for them can be very difficult.

Thirdly, there are additional problems of sharecroppers and tenants, those landless persons or near landless persons who lease in small plots of cultivation land. They are denied several benefits which landowner-cultivators can access. They have to hand over a big share of their meager produce to the landowner but bear most of the costs.

Next there are owner-cultivators or farmers. The bulk of them are small farmers with a low resource base, vulnerable to weather extremes and other adverse situations. Even in normal times they have many problems vis-à-vis getting a fair price for their crop. They often have to resort to distress sale. Accessing government benefits is another problem. Due to wrong and distorted policies, they face escalating farm costs. Deteriorating soil and water conditions and ecological damage have made it very difficult to improve or maintain yields despite spending a lot on inputs. Most of them are in debt.

There is a rich diversity of poor rural artisans and

crafts-persons in India including potters, weavers, leather workers and several others who confront many problems. Covid-19 has ravaged markets for several of their products.

There are several service providers in rural areas like sanitation workers, dhobis, barbers, oil-millers and vendors who suffer from different problems.

There are villagers specializing in animal related work. Due to various reasons those dealing in cattle, camels, goats, sheep and bees and other species have suffered in recent times. Selling products like milk and honey has become difficult, particularly for those outside limited marketing chains. Traditional fisher-folk, whether working in rivers, lakes, ponds or coastal areas too battle increasing problems.

There are nomadic and semi-nomadic groups who have been generally among the most neglected. Their problems went up all the more amid Covid as established patterns of migration and related livelihoods broke down.

Tribal communities have suffered a lot in terms of land alienation, displacement and erosion of forest rights. They have been subjected to many-sided exploitation, including in marketing of non-timber forest produce collected by them.

There are several groups who face serious social discrimination, which sometimes takes the form of violence. This discrimination can be on the basis of caste and increasingly also on the basis of faith or religion. Dalits and Muslims have suffered the most.

Women and girls in villages suffer due to discrimination as well as violence. The limited gains made by girls earlier in education have been badly threatened in Covid times.

Violence against women has increased due to increasing alcoholism. While levels of domestic violence are high, opportunities of women in obtaining paid work has declined.

The growing numbers of unemployed youth face uncertain and troubled times. These intensified due to disruption of normal economic, educational and training work as well as transport after Covid erupted.

5.7 Tribal Land and Forest Rights

Many commentators on land and forest rights, including former senior government officials, have expressed serious concern over the land alienation suffered by tribal farmers and the dilution of their forest rights. While this has led to a serious livelihood crisis among a large number of tribal households, it has caused immense threats to the rich traditional wisdom of tribal communities with respect to farming systems. Their ways protect environment instead of burdening and polluting it. The amazing biodiversity protected, valued and nurtured by them from generation to generation and the respect they accord to nutrition and medicinal value of many plants and herbs growing freely in forests are praiseworthy.

Those who have tried to work closely with tribal farmers and understand their systems have been able to appreciate the wisdom of these systems. They seek to obtain healthy food and meet other basic needs from a mixed system of farms and forests without causing any pollution and in fact nurturing the sustainability of the system in several time-honored ways. Senior scientists like Dr RH Richharia, former director of Central Rice Research Institute, who worked closely with tribal farmers (particularly of Chhattisgarh), testified to their wisdom and perseverance in protecting thousands of varieties through their indigenous systems. This has been increasingly threatened by the thoughtless onslaught of modernity.

This vast knowledge of tribal communities is accompanied by other wisdom relating to weather conditions and adjusting to adverse weather. All this is now needed more than ever in times of climate change. Unfortunately, there is an overwhelming attitude of neglect bordering on contempt towards this traditional expertise. This neglect will prove very costly.

It is by now widely agreed that tribal communities in India have suffered in many cases from extreme injustice in most basic livelihood contexts of farmland and forest rights. In a paper, *Review of Land Reforms During 1950-95,* Sukumar Das, a former senior government official, has written, '.... Land legislation to protect the tribal people has failed to achieve its basic objective. In fact, more than 50 percent of the total land allotted by the government has already been alienated. The state governments taken together have so far allotted 0.47 million hectares of vested land to 0.42 million tribal households whereas 0.31 million hectares of tribal land has been alienated from 0.24 million tribal households of India.'

The overall development strategy pursued by India in recent times has involved ruthless displacement of farmers and rural communities. Due to the higher concentration of mineral and forest wealth as well as hydro-power potential in tribal regions, tribal communities have been affected most adversely by displacement.

Despite the tribals bearing the biggest share of the burden of many-sided displacements and alienation from their land, there was a flicker of new hope when the Scheduled Tribes and Traditional Forest Dwellers Forest Rights Act was passed. This Act hoped to correct the 'historical injustice' caused to farmers.

The background to this injustice was that in colonial times vast areas were arbitrarily declared Forest Department land without any consideration for the rights of people obtaining their livelihood from this land. These people came to be called encroachers and were subjected to all kinds of repression. The stated aim of the FRA was to correct this injustice by devising a procedure to regularize the land holdings cultivated by tribal households.

The procedure provided by the law was that tribals and other traditional forest dwellers would submit claims, these would be examined and, if found correct, legal entitlements will be provided to them. As the entire objective of this law was to correct a historical injustice, it was widely believed that an overwhelming majority of claims will be accepted and tribals/forest dwellers will be in a much better position by receiving entitlements.

But the real picture emerging from the implementation of FRA has been different. Firstly, the number of rejection of claims has been very high. Those whose claim was rejected were often not even informed about it. Secondly, a significant number of deserving allottees have been simply left out as they could not send their claims properly in time. Lastly, even in the case of those whose claims were accepted, often the acceptance was only for a small part of land being cultivated, hence even in acceptance cases the livelihood situation may have been actually eroded.

An immediate review of the implementation of FRA should be taken up and corrections should be introduced. More specifically, the high rate of claim rejections should be brought down significantly. The tendency to reduce land cultivated in most cases should be checked. Those who couldn't get the chance to present their claims should get help to do so.

If despite such a review several tribals and poor farmers involved in disputes with the Forest Department are left out of the scope of this legislation, then in such cases efforts should be made to involve them in tree farming schemes. This way, the objective of increasing tree cover can be reconciled with protecting the livelihood of these people and no evictions will be necessary.

All cases of tribal land alienation should be resolved speedily so that their land is restored to them.

5.8 Issues Likely to Prove Costly

Several countries including India have embarked on a development strategy which emphasizes very rapid and large-scale extraction of minerals, construction of large dams and super highways, massive urbanization and industrial projects. This is equated with development and progress and hence, adequate and proper attention is not given to the social and environmental costs for rural and tribal communities, farmers and pastorals. Ditto for forests and other ecologically important areas (including habitats of so many forms of life), to trees of common areas and orchards, to grazing lands and wetlands, floodplains and coastal areas.

Quite often the best regimes can think of is a compensatory mechanism of planting trees at some other places or giving cash or other compensation to those displaced by big projects. This too is done often in a selective or inadequate way. Such a process adversely affects a large mass who may not be able to produce the required legal documents.

Millions of such displaced people in India have been pushed away from their rural livelihoods while millions more are threatened. The forcible shift away from cleaner, airy rural areas with green fields to congested slums in cities is always painful. Globally, this happens at a much more gigantic level.

The loss of forests and habitats is no less harmful. In times of climate change this is inexcusable. I have at times travelled on highways which local people said were not really needed but involved the thoughtless cutting of thousands of beautiful, magnificent trees with invaluable ecological contributions. Similarly, many dams, mining and industrial projects have been widely criticized.

In many countries, the tendency is to manage things in such a way that the full social and environmental costs are almost never taken into reckoning while clearing projects. Many projects are cleared in highly corrupt systems with big pay-offs tied to various such approvals. It becomes clear why many such decisions are inherently biased against the rural communities and environment protection.

The grave harm done to sustainable rural livelihoods and long-term food security by the diversion of limited fertile farmlands should be resisted. There should be a clear decision that the more fertile land will not be diverted for non-farming use. The remaining natural forests will not be subjected to any further clear felling or submergence or conversion to monoculture plantations.

Crucial Policy Issues

Current farm practices in industrialized countries have created incentives for farmers to use environmentally damaging practices and in many cases penalized farmers for switching to more sustainable practices. The system of farm programme payments in the US has worked against long-term rotations and reduction of chemical inputs. In the European Community, price policies have discouraged production of pulses. Although mixed crop-livestock systems can be the basis for environmentally sustainable farming, distorted price structures have tended to push agriculture in the other direction, toward specialization

—The World Resources Report

6.1 Real Needs and Actual Policy

It is easy to have a very wide agreement on the obvious fact that food and farming is one of the most important sectors of human efforts and needs. But while this should lead to caring and careful attitudes, its importance is being interpreted by powerful forces in a very different way to increase their control and dominance over these systems, starting with seeds and leading all the way to the dining table. A top American official went to the extent of infamously saying bluntly—food is a weapon. This statement, incredibly enough, is often quoted as a sign of strategic wisdom, emanating from the biggest food power.

Yes, it is extremely sad but equally true that the distance between what is needed and what is happening in the food and farming sector worldwide is growing. It is no longer a matter of just increasing distance. It is more true to say that what is needed in this crucial sector is seriously in conflict with what is happening at the policy level.

Most people would agree on what they want from the food and farming system. Firstly, they want it to provide them adequate food which is safe, healthy and nourishing. Secondly, they want this food at a reasonable cost.

Thirdly, they would like to ensure the sustainability and reliability of this system, even in predicted times of adverse weather and climate change. Essential conditions for this like soil health and water availability should be well protected. Next, they would like assured supply of good quality essential raw materials like cotton. Fifthly, farmers and farm workers should get satisfactory income as well as secure, sustainable livelihoods.

Next, they would like to protect environment and biodiversity and health-nourishing conditions of villages. Last but not the least, they would like to protect the welfare of all animals, birds and all life-forms that contribute to our food system.

The ecologically conscious citizens would want farming to contribute more and more to checking climate change.

It is possible to honour these wishes provided farm production and protecting environment are in harmony with each other.

But serious problems arise when big business interests who do not share these aims or regard them much less important wish to control the food and farming sector. They are able to actually strengthen their grip and power over the sector to a very considerable extent, clamping down on the voice of farmers, consumers and environmentalists. They use corrupt lobbying methods to secure the collusion of officials, politicians and 'experts'.

This is the primary reason why official policy, and the laws enacted to promote it are increasingly in conflict with what is actually needed and desired by most people. This is why farmers, consumers, environmentalists and all citizens need to get together to resolve this conflict.

This is the wider context in which the farmers' movement in India and various other campaigns in various countries should be viewed, seen and supported.

6.2 Real Problem and Outward Manifestation

While trying to find sustainable solutions to problems

building up over a long time, it is helpful to keep in mind that the outward manifestation is not necessarily the real problem or its core. This is evident in the context of farming where a number of serious problems have been building up over many decades.

In several places the seeds and crop varieties which had evolved keeping in view the specific agro-ecological conditions have been displaced from the fields. The self-reliance of farming communities in terms of the most basic input of seeds has been lost. If the market provides seeds which grow well only with chemical fertilizers and specific pesticide and herbicide requirements then this has to be followed regardless of the economic costs and health hazards.

These increase pressures on farmers to change the cropping calendar based on new changes imposed from outside. This in turn increases the pressure for mechanization of farming. Small farmers end up investing more than what they can afford in costly machines.

This increases costs of farmers and risks of farmers considerably. Debts can pile up. The problem increases with high interest rates, corruption in credit, sales of products of dubious quality and uses of heavy handed methods to recover loans.

The excessive use of chemical fertilizers, pesticides and herbicides has pushed down the organic content of soil and killed friendly organisms which enhance fertility. Organic matter suffer overall natural fertility declines. Desperate farmers then spend more and more on chemical fertilizers to maintain yields.

Poisonous pesticides kill friendly insects and birds,

including invaluable pollinators, in huge numbers. Harmful targeted pests may develop immunity. Over a period, the factors that contribute to farming bounty without any economic costs decline, resulting in depletion of natural fertility and rising of costs.

The focus of technology-based development leads to neglect of social dimensions of progress. Inequalities have existed for a long time resulting in concentration of land in the hands of a few in many villages. Often there is neglect of sections considered lower in the rural social hierarchy, leading to increased alienation and sometimes even hostility.

Farmers often forget the livelihood needs of landless farm workers while going in for expensive mechanization. The landless become more inclined towards migration based livelihoods. These lead to fissures in community life as various sections form their own wider support groupings. In some cases, there is a rise in unaffordable wasteful expenditure and, what is worse, higher consumption of liquor and other substance abuse.

When frustrations increase due to economic problems or social alienation/humiliation, these can be easily directed towards religious fundamentalism, communalism and sectarianism. Another outlet in crime.

All these create a distressing and tense situation when farmers do not get a fair price or get less than expected or promised price for their produce. This may happen due to cheating by business interests or a failure of the government resulting from inefficiency and failure to allocate adequate resources for this purchase and necessary infrastructure.

If the government gives inadequate support to ensure fair price for all, the bigger and more influential farmers corner the bulk of the benefits.

One, they take advantage of the inability of small farmers to wait their turn in government purchase. The bigger farmers or traders may buy the small farmers' produce at a lesser price and then sell it to the government in the name of small farmers. Hence, government records may continue to show significant procurement from small farmers while the reality may be quite different.

As the immediate problem is the denial or delay of what is perceived to be a just and remunerative price, the entire focus may shift to this for getting some immediate relief. Or it may shift to writing off or atleast postponing some loans or interest payments due from farmers. This is a response to the most obvious and visible current manifestation of the problem and not to the many-sided, complex realities of the wider, deeper problem of rural distress.

It is important to realize this wider dimension of the existing problems. A much more holistic, comprehensive and deeper response is needed at several levels.

6.3 Trapped in Unsustainable Systems

Governments in many countries grapple with the challenge of retaining the support of farmers considered important in electoral politics. At the same time, many governments work under the impact of powerful business interests. From the narrow point of view of such governments, the skill is in somehow managing to keep both business interests and farmers happy. This is difficult. So, what they try to do is to keep a smaller number of influential farmers on their side. These are generally the bigger farmers and their leaders.

In the process some sort of compromise is worked out in which the big farmers and big business are major beneficiaries. Medium and small farmers also get some relief from time to time. In turn, the regime gets a big political support base. Outwardly things look stable. However, in the process of achieving this, often the considerations of sustainability and environment protection are sacrificed.

The short term higher benefits are sought to be secured by a more extractive system which tries to get more and more out of nature while pushing aside inconvenient questions of soil harm, water depletion and environment destruction. Many periods of higher farm productivity and higher cash receipts are those in which heavy damage to sustainability and environment is caused. In addition, the interests of the least influential and poorest section of landless rural households too are sacrificed.

This compromise and the attempt to create a consensus on an unsustainable and extractive system is highly unstable as the problems caused by destruction of environment and depletion of soil fertility and water resources catches up.

Rich countries have often tried to find a way out by pushing the burden on poorer countries using unfair trade practices, patent laws, seed and input control, technological and other means of domination, promoting multinational companies and imposing agreements which indulge in dirty tricks.

On the other hand, rural regimes of poorer countries have fewer options when the crisis catches up with a highly extractive farming systems. Still, skillful politicians bide their time till next elections, using relief and populist measures in the meantime.

Problems get more difficult when big business interests become greedier and try to obtain too much in a short time or when politicians come so much under their influence that they fail to reconcile the interests of farmers with those of business.

What has happened in recent times is that the unsustainability created by highly extractive systems has increased. At the same time, the greed of big business and their ability to influence governments too has gone up. This is leading to further discontent and conflict.

Ultimately it remains to be seen whether solutions will be sought within the existing distortions of non-sustainability and many-sided ecological ruin on the one hand and neglect of the poorest and most vulnerable sections on the other hand or whether solutions outside the current paradigm of development thinking will also be considered.

In the prevailing condition, the most important questions are not even considered.

For example, if high-water guzzling sugarcane monocultures grown with large quantities of chemical fertilizers are tied to providing the raw material for highly polluting sugar factories and liquor distilleries, the question of a mixed cropping, staple food crop growing alternative based on agro-ecology and ensuring food security is not even considered. The struggle remains confined generally to getting better price for sugarcane or ensuring early payment of pending dues.

Politicians win elections by clearing pending dues in an election year or including this as a key election promise. Hence, when the struggles of farmers take place, often the highly unsustainable and self-destructive paradigm of development is not even questioned.

Sometimes 'solutions' are found which leave untouched the basic unsustainable situation or even worsen it as long as big business interests, sections of influential farmers and the government find a compromise acceptable to them. But such compromises only worsen the crisis.

If the focus is just on ensuring a high and definite price within a system that harms sustainability, this will be an incentive for accentuating the distorted system.

It is therefore vital to keep re-emphasizing the most basic issues—creating more sustainable, ecologically protective and resilient systems and protecting the interests of the weakest sections. This can contribute in some measure to the emergence of more just and protective solutions.

6.4 Watershed Moment for Farm Policy

It is important to know that the world is in the middle of a watershed moment for farm policy. So is India. The most critical issue to consider now and in coming years relates to climate change and related environmental problems which constitute a survival crisis for the life-nurturing conditions of our planet.

This is widely predicted to bring more erratic and extreme weather and more frequent and intense disasters, worsening water shortages. Hence, well-planned efforts are needed to prepare farming and farmers to meet these adverse situations effectively. It is a huge challenge to protect farmers and maintain adequate food and other essential crop production for an increasing population. All this calls for careful and well-planned efforts.

There is another very important way in which climate change relates to farm policy. As the world searches desperately for processes to check climate change and reduce greenhouse gas emissions, one of the most effective approaches of achieving this is by making suitable changes in the farm and food system.

Farmers and farm workers, helped, encouraged and guided to do the right things can make the biggest contribution. The most gratifying aspect scientists as well as grassroots workers, farmers and activists are discovering is that the efforts needed to face climate change are along the very lines as the attempts to reduce GHG emissions.

1. Firstly, climate change is an extremely important context for farm policy change now and in future years.
2. Climate change brings huge threats but it is possible to change farming in ways to prepare well for this and minimize damage.
3. It is also possible to make changes in farm and food system to check climate change and reduce GHG emissions.
4. So, why can't we move rapidly in this direction? Unfortunately, the most dominant trend of recent decades has been the growing domination of the food and farming system by big business interests including multinationals and billionaires. They are the biggest

hurdle in making the desirable changes.

However, the good news is that changes indicated in points 2 and 3 can be brought in ways that help small and medium farmers and family farms all over the world. This will also help farm workers and promote welfare of farm animals and all forms of life.

5. It is extremely important to resist and remove the dominance of big business interests in the food and farming systems.
6. When this dominance goes, we clear the path for a farm policy based on genuinely desirable objectives.
7. Three of these are protection of sustainable (protecting soil, water, pollinators) satisfactory livelihood of small and medium farmers and family farms, production of adequate safe and healthy food and welfare of all forms of life.
8. It is possible to adapt to climate change and to check climate change while at the same time achieve the objectives in point 7. All desirable objectives move in the same direction without any contradiction.

Now is the time to make the critical changes mentioned above, keeping in view the fast increasing threat of climate change and the acute crisis of small and medium farmers. Both problems can be resolved together by appropriate policy changes.

All that has been stated above regarding the world is equally true for India, with the addition that farmer discontent is peaking and farmer organizations are yearning for solutions. So, this is the right time for farm policy changes, starting with the repeal of the three controversial farm laws. The country should then move in the direction of ecologically protective farming and more caring policies for small farmers and landless farm workers.

6.5 Resolving Farming Crisis Urgent, Difficult

In initial phase of farmers' movement and negotiations, the non-acceptance of the farmers' demand to repeal the three farm laws was touted as the most important reason for the impasse. The truth is this could have been accepted by any sympathetic government. This would not have cost the government any expenditure. The fact that the immediate implementation of the laws is not on the cards makes it all the more easier to accept the demand.

Even a quick reading of the laws will convince most unbiased observers that these were not needed and would have worsened the farming crises if implemented. The govt's initial adamancy indicated it was to a larger and related agenda of farm development (wrongly described as reform) based on crony capitalism. This is harmful for sustainable livelihoods and food security as well as biodiversity and environment.

In fact there are powerful interests which propagate an even more aggressive shift towards corporatization. Two frequently named billionaires and MNCs are behind this. This is seen in the strong pressures to introduce GM food crops. These efforts were quite near to succeeding but for the determined resistance put up by certain groups, including a relatively small but honest part of the Sangh Parivar. But efforts at pushing GM crops may be revived again.

The Union government is right when it says that its keenness on corporatization is shared by several opposition parties or at least by some important leaders within these parties. It is not difficult to find instances of present day opposition leaders who made strong statements in the past promoting corporatization of farming. The first big boost for corporatization in farming and reduction of rural self-reliance was provided by the green revolution. By and large the Congress party still sees the green revolution as a major achievement. Left to his own devices, it is likely that the former Prime Minister, Dr Manmohan Singh, would also have favoured greater corporatization of farming including, in all probability, the introduction of GM food crops.

As far as the pro-establishment experts of farming who dominate the media discourse are concerned, they take the green revolution for granted. They would be happy to see GM food crops and react with shock if anyone suggests any alternative to a corporatization-led path of agricultural development. As far as land reforms and land redistribution for the landless is concerned, the establishment experts would rather not mention it at all (except to oppose it).

The leading political parties prefer to avoid the subject of land redistribution altogether. Indeed, even some of the farmer organizations (not all) are not keen on this.

The overall situation is that most of the influential forces are likely to follow a farm development path not capable of resolving the farming and rural crisis. A very firm commitment to land reforms, ecologically protective farming and rural self-reliance is needed. This agenda is not accepted sincerely by any of the influential forces today.

There is no compelling evidence of a firm commitment of even a major section of the farmers movement and the Left to this.

This is why a satisfactory resolving of the farming and related crisis at present is very difficult. At the same time, it is extremely important to resolve this crisis. India faces this challenge on the largest scale compared to any other country. Saving sustainable livelihoods based on farming and related activities is more crucial. The challenges of malnutrition, rapid loss of soil health and water resource, loss of biodiversity, natural pollinators and organisms important for healthy farming, worsening disasters and weather extremes all are present on a massive scale.

Resolving the farming crisis in the best possible way in India will be extremely beneficial for the entire world. Because India can also become a role model of protecting sustainable livelihoods and food security in times of climate change.

However, a firm commitment for this is difficult to obtain from any of the most influential forces in the country. In this depressing situation, efforts to promote initiatives in the right direction should continue.

6.6 Most Valuable Wealth Few Use Properly

Gold has long been considered the most important form of wealth. Diamonds are another. When oil became the most widely used source of energy, then people started referring to oil as the black gold. At various times since then, different important minerals have been highlighted as very valuable.

But the more these minerals are extracted, the lesser their value remains with the country. What is more, the very process of their extraction often involves so much damage to the environment. The profit from their mining and trade is often concentrated in the hands of a few rich persons and entities. The wealth of these minerals is often concentrated in a few regions but there is no assurance at all the people there will benefit from this. In fact, extraction of the more valuable minerals has frequently involved much violence, displacement and hazards, often directed at local people.

On the other hand, there is another form of wealth available in abundance. The more care with which it is used, the more its value can increase and people can go on using it without reducing its worth. For all who recognize its value and use it properly, benefits will accrue forever. This most abundant wealth accessible to all is soil.

Till about a century ago there was widespread appreciation of the great worth of soil. A reflection of this was that whenever one had to take a pledge of honour and self-respect, this was done in the name of soil (*mitti ki saugandh*). This was no empty talk. It was matched by a lot of care and commitment to maintaining the quality of soil. But as people started giving less attention to its care, the references to soil in daily talk also suffered a degradation.

The most important contribution of soil is associated with providing food. The more care we give to soil and protect its natural fertility, the more assured we can be of getting healthy, safe and nutritious food on sustainable basis. The less care we give, the lesser will be the ability of the soil.

Soil is home to billions of creatures such as earthworms and micro-organisms, very welcome and useful inhabitants of this planet who contribute to its welfare. They demand no feed or fodder from human beings; they merely ask for a right to live in the soil undisturbed. But human beings have denied even this basic right to their most undemanding friends. By indiscriminate use of agro-chemicals and in other ways, people have been killing and destroying billions of these humble beings.

Good care of soil is also important to ensure adequate availability of water. If porosity and stability of soil is maintained (earthworms can again be very helpful in this), then rainwater and moisture can be better conserved.

The importance of care and protection of soil has increased in times of climate change. The key to maintaining the soil's natural fertility is its organic content, obtained by decomposition of various biological materials including fallen leaves, other plant residues and excreta of various life forms particularly those which dwell in soil. Since soil is spread all over, with better care and increase of organic content over many years, we can not only contribute much to improving the prospects of healthy food and satisfying sustainable livelihoods but can also help check climate change.

This protection of soil should be confined not just to rural areas. In urban areas, the craze for indiscriminate concretization should be given up. There should be more green spaces and gardens created in natural ways.

Soil is thus the most important wealth of any country. While millions of people are willing to slog, cheat, rob or even kill for gold, diamonds and cash, unfortunately the realization of soil's importance does not get adequate attention. Recent decades have witnessed not just increasing neglect but relentless destruction of soil and soil-organisms. The decreasing number of farmers and gardeners are being scorned. Family farms and farming communities which alone are capable of taking care of soil are being pushed aside by big corporate interests. The latter, with their heavy machines and agro-chemicals, mount nothing less than an assault on soil health and on soil organisms.

6.7 Cruelty To Creatures Who Serve

Guess who has served humanity in the most valuable way with the greatest continuity and most selflessly? Answer: earthworms. They have been performing their role without seeking anything in return. Their selfless service continues 24x7.

While humans allowed earthworms more or less alone, to carry out their selfless activities for the greater part of history, in the last few decades or so nothing less than a genocide has been inflicted on them. Billions of earthworms have been lost or have perished under the assault of agro-chemicals and related factors.

Earthworms were called builders of human civilization by Charles Darwin and for good reason. Their contribution as well as the role played by various other organisms and micro-organisms for building up the organic content of soil and for maintaining its natural fertility has been immense. They cannot be replaced by anything or anyone else. Earthworms make this contribution as part of their routine activities such as their feeding and excretion and movements within soil. They need no feeding or help from human beings.

The continuing movements of billions of earthworms also help to maintain and increase the porosity of soil and improve its capacity to absorb and retain water and moisture. This is very helpful during rains to prevent overflow and floods and later to provide relief when there is no rain.

By using poisonous agro-chemicals and following other practices which harm soil, human beings have caused a colossal decline in the number of earthworms and soil-dwelling organisms. As the World Resources Report has pointed out, using heavy doses of chemical pesticides in intensive monocultures causes wholesale elimination of helpful soil dwelling insects and microorganisms that build soil and plant nutrition.

The unmistakable and unforgivable reality of recent trends in agriculture has been that the best friends of humanity and of farmers in particular have been killed in billions, thanks to big business interests.

It is another aspect of reductionist thinking that this harm can be undone by bringing in earthworms from another place as manure. Living beings cannot be reduced to manure. One species of earthworms cannot be expected to play the same vibrant role in another type of distant land. There is no alternative to re-creating healthy soil where earthworms and micro-organisms can return on their own.

Unfortunately, the great reduction in earthworms has taken place at a time when we need them and their services the most. In times of climate change, the organic content of soil becomes even more important as in addition to maintaining fertility it helps in absorbing carbon. The porosity of soil is critical to face droughts and floods.

So revival, protection and care of earthworms and soil dwelling organisms should be accepted as an important and a pressing responsibility, not only in village farms but in urban gardens as well.

6.8 Government, Farmers, Sustainable System

Farming in India has been increasingly discussed globally in the context of the on-going farmers' movement. India has a special position as nearly two thirds of the population still lives in rural areas. Therefore, whatever policy options it adopts for farming are considered important.

It is understandable that when a democratic and determined movement of farmers exerted its strength to check corporatization being pushed by the Union Government which tried to pass three farm laws, this attracted very wide attention the world over.

Given the strong opposition of the farmers, criticism of the government for earlier refusing to consider the repeal of the farm laws is evident. Organizations of many sections including Dalit landless farm workers, students and youth, women as well as workers have extended support to the farmers. Aspects of the movement include inter-faith harmony, unity of farmers from different regions and castes, and enthusiastic participation of volunteers.

Having said this, however, limitations of this movement should be pointed out. For a justice based, eco-protective and sustainable resolution of the farming crisis and for sustainable availability of healthy and safe food, it is important to make a firm commitment to land reforms, particularly redistribution of at least some land to the poorest and landless. Secondly, it is equally necessary to take a pledge to ecologically protective farming systems (social agro-ecology). Going by the official pronouncements of the farmers' movement, no such commitment is visible.

On the strength of the evidence available, this farmers' movement is also not prepared to sail towards a just, healthy, ecologically protective, secure and sustainable food and farming system. This needs to be stated firmly and clearly so that the urgency of the need for an alternative paradigm, different from the one presented so far, is not forgotten.

The reasons why the protesting farmers should continue to get our support are many. By opposing the farm laws, this movement seeks to prevent the further decline of our already unsustainable and unjust farming system. It provides an important point of courageous and well-organized resistance to increasingly authoritarian trends and forces. It promotes national unity and communal harmony and increases social mobilization of rural women. It creates a window of dialogue to make farmers more caring about landless households, particularly the Dalits.

Food Processing Needs Improvements

The quantitative loss in the case of cereals alone may amount to not less than eight million tonnes. The qualitative loss is even more staggering because the portions of the grain that are removed in refinement are many times richer in quality, proteins, fats, minerals such as iron and phosphorous, and vitamins such as thiamine, nicotinic acid, riboflavin, and, in some cases, also vitamin A, in the form of carotene, than the portions that are retained and consumed by us. These are precisely the nutrients in which the average Indian diet is woefully deficient.

—L Ramachandran in *Food Planning*

7.1 Check Wasteful Food Processing

While agriculture has been much in discussion, the related work of food processing has hardly received any attention. This is despite the fact that there is a huge scope for providing millions of rural jobs. At the same time, one can improve the nutrition situation significantly by moving from present-day big-business controlled food processing to food crop and other crop processing in small and cottage rural industries.

At present, a lot of unnecessary and possibly harmful additives are being used. Also, wasteful practices are actually removing nutrients on a large-scale from the most staple foods. The technologies used for obtaining rice from paddy involve a lot of wastage of grain. What is more, the part of grain which is wasted is the one which is the most nutritious.

According to an expert L Ramchandran, who has made detailed estimates of the loss suffered in the process of refining cereals in his book '*Food Planning*,' 'The quantitative loss in the case of cereals alone may amount to not less than eight million tonnes. The qualitative loss is even more staggering because the portions of the grain that are removed in refinement are many times richer in quality, proteins, fats, minerals such as iron and phosphorous, and vitamins such as thiamine, nicotinic acid, riboflavin, and, in some cases, also vitamin A, in the form of carotene, than the portions that are retained and consumed by us. These are precisely the nutrients in which the average Indian diet is woefully deficient.'

Another major source of loss of nutrients is the hydrogenation of oils. Hydrogenation changes most of the unsaturated fats into saturated fat, which consumed in excess can cause harm. Unsaturated fats, especially some of the poly unsaturated fats, are important in nutrition and play a protective role against cardiovascular disease and other ailments. In the words of Ramchandran, 'in hydrogenation, what is good and necessary is changed into what is not necessary and may be harmful.'

There has been a big increase in recent years in the number and quantity of additives used by the food processing industry including flavours, colours, emulsifiers, preservatives and an amazing range of other additives. The combinations of additives may react with each other and with foods to produce new chemical substances. A number of health hazards have been blamed on several additives and their combinations.

This gigantic waste is perpetuated and accentuated with the flooding of junk food. Simultaneously, talented and skilled traditional processors of food languish in neglect and face loss of livelihood. There is a crying need for cottage and small-scale food industries in villages, led by women and self-help groups and co-operatives, which can take up the processing of cereals, millets, pulses, vegetables, fruits, milk and milk products, spices and honey. This will generate millions of jobs, encourage creativity and entrepreneurship while ensuring healthy, tasty, safe and nutritious food.

7.2 Diversion of Food Crops to Industrial Use

There has been an increasing tendency worldwide to divert a lot of high-nutrition food crops to industrial uses. In addition, many food crops are not being used as staple foods but instead processed in complicated ways to serve as raw materials for the food industry in different forms. What impact will this have on food security and food safety?

If a huge quantity of staple food crops is diverted to industrial use, there can be a shortage despite a reported increase in production. Food safety can be compromised by highly complex processing, involving many chemicals, whose health impacts are not realized or else are actively hidden or understated.

To give one example, a significant amount of corn has been steadily shifted to high-fructose corn syrup (HFCS) which has several uses in food industry and industrial uses as well. How is HFCS obtained from corn? Raj Patel has described this in his widely acclaimed book, *Stuffed and Starved*, 'Through a process known as wet milling, corn is first dried, sorted and dipped in sulphurous acid; the germ of the seed is removed, washed, filtered, spun and then heated with weak hydrochloric acid to make corn syrup. At this point, the resulting mixture, once cleansed and treated, is about three-quarters as sweet as sugar. To raise the sweetness level, the amount of fructose is raised by reacting it with enzymes, and then it is made sweeter still by distilling and concentrating it. The resulting 80-90 percent fructose is then diluted to get the industry standard 55 percent high-fructose corn syrup.'

We leave it to the readers to decide how proper and safe it is to process a high nutrition staple food crop this way. An additional issue is that once such industrial uses become more important, crop breeding is increasingly used to switch over to those varieties of food crops which are more amenable to industrial processing. Hence, availability of nourishing, healthy and safe food suffers at several levels.

There is a growing worldwide trend towards heavy diversion of food crops for use as bio-fuels. While there is a huge diversion from food to fuel, the actual loss to food security can be even more if more fertile lands suitable for food are diverted to biofuel and used in unsustainable ways for monocultures of biofuel crops. Biofuels can contribute to reducing use of fossil fuels; if fossil fuel intensive inputs are used to produce biofuels, abandoning organic production of food in ways which reduce or absorb GHG emissions, then the net result may not be useful to check climate change.

Writing about trends and prospects in bio-fuel in India, Petroleum Minister Dharmendra Pradhan wrote in *The Hindustan Times,* 'Ethanol supplies have improved from 380 million litres in 2013-14 to 1.89 billion litres (1,890 million litres) in 2019. Offers of about 3.5 billion litres from both sugar/molasses and grain-based distilleries are expected this year.' In addition, he refers to a recent decision to 'utilize surplus rice available with the Food Corporation of India and maize as an additional source of feedstock for ethanol production.'

Clearly, there is a need for concern at a time of widespread hunger and malnutrition among the people regarding the transfer of staple food crops to industrial uses and related factors.

7.3 Food Processing is Critical

While fierce debates rage on agriculture, the critical role of food processing is often neglected. This can prove costly as the people of Mexico discovered much to their cost.

In the early 1990s, a heated discussion went on in Mexico regarding the desirability of joining (with the US and Canada) the North American Free Trade Agreement (NAFTA). It was generally agreed that as corn (maize) was a staple crop of Mexico, most small farmers in the country growing this crop will lose rather heavily due to the import of cheaper, subsidized wheat from the US. To counter this, the supporters of NAFTA argued that this will bring cheaper food to consumers. After all, the number of consumers was much larger than the number of corn farmers. This argument won the day and Mexico's journey with NAFTA started on January 1.

Predictably over a million farmers were driven off their land. The rush of the displaced farmers to cities led to fall in industrial wages. But what about the promised benefits of cheaper food to consumers? This did not work out. Instead, the price of staple food increased steeply. What exactly happened?

Corn as the staple food is consumed in the form of tortillas in Mexico. The price of tortillas is related to the price of corn flour. In this market, food processing is highly concentrated in the hands of big business. At that time, just two leading players controlled almost 97 percent of the industrial corn flour market. They were getting increasing government subsidies but still they connived to increase the price of tortillas sharply in post NAFTA years. Probably as part of the same NAFTA driven 'reforms', the government cut back on its own arrangements for making available cheaper tortillas and other staple food. With disrupted livelihoods, declining income and higher price of staple food, poverty increased. Female headed households witnessed poverty rate increase of up to 50 percent.

Could things have been different if the work of obtaining flour from corn and then preparing tortillas was also in the hands of farmers or other villagers or nearby small towns close to them? The least that can be said is that if this food-processing was also in the hands of ordinary people, the chances of avoiding arbitrary increase in price would have been much higher.

The experience of Mexico is important for countries like India where too food processing is increasingly passing from cottage-scale to big industry. This change has never received the same importance as agriculture per se. This neglect can prove very costly.

While researching this subject, I was looking for cottage-scale rice-milling in villages but did not find any. A friend, Jagdish Pradhan (of Sahbhagi Vikash Abhiyan or SVA in Odisha), told me the reason why such units are so difficult to locate now in the land of Mahatma Gandhi. He said setting up such small units was banned some time back in India. India taking the Mexico road? But my friend also gave me a good news. He said they were keen to set up such cottage-scale mills in their programme area in Western Odisha. They decided to challenge the ban. Finding some sympathetic officials, they were able to obtain a reversal of this highly arbitrary decision. This is good news but the question is why was such an arbitrary ban placed in the first place?

Some time back there were reports in Delhi of some cottage-scale wheat mills facing closure on the pretext of anti-pollution and urban sealing. Fortunately, many such wheat mills have survived although their share in total wheat processing has come down heavily. In hilly areas, gharats or water mills are fabled for the good quality of their flour, whether of wheat or corn or various millets, as the grinding takes place at a slower pace. But even the water mills have shown a sharp decline in numbers.

Mangal Singh, a talented but neglected farmer scientist from Bundelkhand, has invented a Mangal Turbine which can lift water without diesel or electricity from streams and rivulets. Less known is the fact that this can easily have add-ons for milling various grains and millets. What such traditional as well as recent efforts reveal is that if food processing remains in the hands of rural communities, there is always room for creativity leading to better designs and efficiency.

Yet another advantage is better nutrition for rural and small town consumers as well as for farm and dairy animals. The residues of village-level processing of grain, millets and oilseeds are likely to become available for consumption of local animals. This is in contrast to the big industry processing where residues like oilcakes and bran enter the wider market to be purchased by those who can afford to pay. In practice, this leads to the export of much of this, denying much needed nutrition to farm and dairy animals in India.

Mahatma Gandhi realized all this and accorded a lot of importance to village-level processing of food and cotton crops. Despite tremendous potential for the creativity of villagers and particularly women, despite the availability of excellent rural skills, despite the clear possibility of generating millions of creative and sustainable jobs, this path has been abandoned.

It is still not too late to return to it as there will be tremendous benefits of human and animal nutrition, availability of cheaper and more healthy food as well as employment generation. Farmer households will benefit much from this diversification of their livelihoods and market closer to home.

7.4 Liquor Production & Consumption and Food Security

There have been several reports about the adverse impact of high levels of meat production and consumption on food production. For example, it is known that seven kg of grain, or more is used to produce one kg of beef in intensive systems. At the same time, massive amounts of water are used, all this has an adverse impact on food security. Unfortunately, similar adverse impacts of increasing alcohol consumption on food security have not received due attention.

As liquor consumption zooms, more and more fertile land is used to grow raw materials for the industry. Often various crops are grown in ways, that can be supplied directly to the liquor industry. Thus, a lot of fertile land is taken away from food production. Liquor being a high profit industry, it is hardly surprising that land is diverted to meet the needs of the liquor industry.

In countries like India and China where liquor intake

and production has increased in a big way, there is a significant diversion of fertile land from producing food to producing (raw material for) liquor.

There has been an increasing trend of diverting highly nutritious fruits like apples and plums in some hill areas from direct consumption to processing liquor as this brings higher profits. In some areas known for high production of apples, children from poor households hardly eat the fruit as it is used in making expensive wines.

In addition, sometimes in government storages, grain is conveniently allowed to rot by corrupt persons with a view to sell it at a cheap price to the liquor industry. This denies availability of food to those who need it the most.

Another way in which food security is impacted is at the level of rising consumption of liquor in poor households. Much to the distress of women and children, men in many such families insist on consuming liquor. The net result is that the food and nutrition situation in poor households is further affected.

A lot of water is diverted for making liquor or for irrigating water-intensive crops meant for the liquor industry even though there is increasing water shortage for drinking and for irrigating food crops.

A report in '*India Today*' by Kiran Tare from Marathwada region said, 'Indiscriminate release of water for sugarcane cultivation and alcohol production has depleted the (water) reservoirs. There are some 200 distilleries in Aurangabad which use enormous quantities of potable water.' This was reported at the time of a serious water scarcity in the area.

In other areas water situation is threatened by wine

production and an increase in grape production to feed wine units. The *Economist* journal reported that 960 litres of water are used for every litre of wine.

There are reports of serious pollution of rivers and water sources due to effluents released by distilleries. The distilleries also spread foul smell, hindering farm work in nearby villages.

What is the total impact of the diversion of huge quantities of potable water to distilleries and the pollution of water sources by effluents released by distilleries? This should be assessed in well-planned water audits.

India leads the world in rising liquor consumption. This has more than doubled between 1995 and 2016. According to WHO projections for 2025, the increase in liquor consumption from 1995 to 2025 will be 3 to 4 times in India. The discussion so far has been on the disastrous health and social impact of this increase. We also need to know the food and water impact.

Many Aspects of Improving Nutrition

A single meal may contain a cocktail of 12 to 16 additives. The combinations of additives may react with each other and with foods to produce new chemical substances. A wide range of health hazards has been reported for an equally wide variety of food additives.

—The London Food Commission

8.1 Widen Paradigm of Nutrition Debate

The nutrition situation in India is shocking. There is an increasing tendency among powerful commercial interests to push their narrow selfish interests in the name of improving the nutrition situation. Sometimes these interests try to push artificial additives or advocate risky GM crops or try to sell certain products. The funds of a high profile nutrition programme in India have been widely used to buy smart phones for nutrition workers.

It is surprising that many government and international agencies are quite supportive towards such narrow selfish use of nutrition needs. Hence, funds badly needed for providing food to undernourished and malnourished get diverted to dubious and sometimes hazardous uses. Such trends should be checked, as also all other corruption in nutrition programs.

Even the serious and well-intentioned debate has assumed a narrow focus in recent times. There is an overwhelming emphasis on the various nutrition schemes, particularly ICDS (Anganwadi) and mid-day meals as also supportive ones like POSHAN, sabla and matru-vandana, besides the public distribution system (PDS).

There is no doubt that these schemes need higher budgetary resources and other reforms. This is also the more obvious, measurable, way of taking forward nutrition. This can be monitored in statistical figures. With their huge reach in India, these schemes are important (despite their temporary closure or setback in Covid times). But to carry out the overall discussion on nutrition mostly in the context of these schemes is not correct. Other critical factors need to be considered.

Ultimately, nutrition depends on whether or not households have the capacity to access, produce or buy nutritious wholesome balanced food for all family members. This depends a lot on equality and justice in society. This is the most important determinant of nutrition. For example, in many villages where hunger and malnutrition exists, this can be reduced drastically simply by more equal distribution of land.

But this is often not even discussed in the context of the nutrition debate. Payment of fair wage, protected and well-paid livelihoods, some form of employment/income guarantee, all these are very important factors in ensuring much better nutrition. But above all an overall system based on equality and justice is most important. Gender justice and equality are also needed. Nutrition is better when the girl child gets the same importance as the boy or when a woman has to right to tell her husband and ensure he obeys!—that limited money available will be spent on fruits and not on liquor.

Secondly, systems capable of producing and making available adequate, diverse, nourishing, safe and healthy staple foods at affordable price are vitally important. This implies (speaking for now in the context of vegetarian food) that clean drinking/cooking water, cereals, millets, oilseeds, legumes, vegetables, fruits, milk and milk products, salt and spices, sugar and jaggery of proper quality should be available in such quantities as to meet the nutrition needs of all people. We are very far from fulfilling this requirement.

Thirdly, protection of environment—in particular soil, water, bio-diversity, pollinators, pastures, forests—is critical to maintain food security in sustainable food production systems. Natural mixed forests have been the repository of so much high nutritious food available for free. This is being lost rapidly.

It is only when we bring in all these and other factors that we can have a proper, comprehensive, holistic understanding of why nutrition in a society is improving or declining, and what needs to be done for sustainable, firmly rooted, broad-based food and nutrition security.

8.2 Multi-Disciplinary Approach on Crucial Issues

The importance of a multi-disciplinary approach to understanding crucial issues is well established both at academic and policy levels. But we need to ask: Is this being neglected frequently in public discourse and, perhaps, even at policy and academic levels?

One reason for this unintentional neglect is that public discourse and, to some extent, even policy are influenced a lot by what appears in media. This is generally driven by what is more in news at a particular time. A multi-disciplinary approach is likely to get easily neglected. In academic fields there is more and more specialization. This is understandable to some extent but this should have been accompanied by renewed emphasis on keeping in mind multi-disciplinary aspects as well. This has not taken place to the extent needed.

Let us take the issue of nutrition. This is influenced by various nutrition schemes. Adequacy of budget allocation, the state of their functioning, involvement of people and related aspects. Another important factor is – to what extent is food denied to many in villages where food is produced because they do not have any farmland? To what extent is land inequality a cause for hunger and malnutrition? How many percentage of people have the income to afford a nutritionally balanced diet? To what extent is non-payment of a fair wage responsible for this?

Even among those sections who have the capacity, how many are not utilizing this properly due to liquor addiction (or other substance abuse)? To what extent is this issue a question of gender disparity? Women are generally keen to check liquor consumption but their voice may not be heard in a situation of male dominance. To what extent is food distributed unequally on gender basis in an overall situation of food scarcity in a household?

To what extent is food production or agriculture system responsive to growing the crops most needed for meeting nutrition needs of a society? To what extent is the food processing and trade system responsive to this? Is adequate consideration given to food safety and to retaining nutrition content of naturally produced food? Is adequate importance given to soil health, water conservation and various sustainability aspects? Is food available in market and ration shops safe and healthy? How important is the role of a public distribution system? To what extent does it meet the needs of a balanced nutrition? Is the availability of raw food (freshly plucked or forest food) diminishing in providing nutrition?

The above is only a partial list of the various factors which influence nutrition. Many of these have experienced fast changes in recent decades in India. To understand nutrition in India we need to comprehensively understand the changing role of all these factors. This calls for a highly multi-disciplinary approach.

8.3 Soil Health and Nutrition

While the critical importance of soil health for good farming is widely recognized, one aspect demanding adequate attention is the link between soil health and nutrition of crops. This needs to be explored further. A note by the Food and Agriculture Organization (FAO) titled '*Healthy Soils Produce Healthy Crops*' states that soil quality is directly related to food quality and quantity.

It is known that excessive use of chemical fertilizers causes a loss of flavour of food. What is less realized is that it can also cause a loss of nutritive value and even create serious health problems. According to prominent nutrition expert C Gopalan, 'The use of high analysis chemical fertilisers, which is part of the modern intensive agricultural technology, had not always gone hand-in-hand with appropriate measures for soil testing and soil replenishment, with the result that, as shown by the studies of FAO (1982), there are disturbing evidences of micronutrient depletion of soils in some areas; these are likely to be eventually reflected in impaired nutritive value of food-grains grown in such soils'.

Such a clear opinion of a senior nutritionist should not be taken lightly. It is not just a question of nutrition value being impaired. Serious health hazards are also involved when soil health is badly harmed by excessive use of agro-chemicals.

Richard Douthwaite has written in his book *The Growth Illusion*, 'Nitrogenous fertilisers can raise the amount of nitrate in the final crop to four or five times the level found in the compost-growing equivalent, while at the same time cutting vitamin C and dry matter levels. This change is potentially serious, since nitrates can be turned into powerful carcinogenic nitrosamines by bacteria found in the mouth, while vitamin C has been shown to protect against cancers.'

While organic matter in the soil, the product of on-side biological decomposition, provides balanced nutrition to soil, unbalanced nutrition provided by various kinds of chemical fertilizers can never equal this. The deficiency of some micro nutrient or the other then keeps emerging. Attempts are made to make up for this by various artificial additives mixed in food. But artificial additives cannot equal the nutrition provided by natural wholesome food grown in healthy soil. In addition, some additives or their excess are also harmful for health.

There has been a major increase in recent years in the number and quantity of additives used by the food processing industry. These include flavours, colours, emulsifiers, preservatives and an amazing range of other additives. The London Food Commission noted in 1988 that about 3,800 additives were used to perform about a hundred functions. Only about a tenth of the additives were subject to government control. The Commission wrote, 'A single meal may contain a cocktail of 12 to 16 additives. The combinations of additives may react with each other and with foods to produce new chemical substances.' A wide range of health hazards has been reported for an equally wide variety of food additives.

The link between soil health and nutrition should be better explored. It is futile to first create nutrition deficiency in staple food and then try to make this up by artificial additives.

Improvements in Crop Procurement

When various crops are being harvested, the government should procure a part of the staple food crops right there in the village at a fair and just price. This procurement should be enough to meet the needs of various staple foods by the public distribution system and nutrition schemes (ICDS or Anganwadi, mid-day meals, sabla scheme for adolescent girls) of the village community. The purchase should be somewhat in excess of exact need so to provide also for an emergency stock within the village.

—Bharat Dogra

9.1 Reforms that Improve Crop Procurement

Procurement of various crops from farmers at a fair price by the government is an integral part of the farm and food system of India. This can be reformed in various ways - reducing costs while improving income of farmers and overall food security.

When various crops are harvested, the government should procure a part of the staple food crops right there in the village at a fair and just price. This procurement should be enough to meet the needs of various staple foods by the public distribution system and nutrition schemes of the village community. The purchase should be somewhat in excess of exact need to provide for an emergency stock within the village.

Small farmers should get priority. A higher premium payment should be made for healthy food grown using organic/natural methods and avoiding dangerous chemicals. The payment to farmers at a fair price should be made immediately. As a wide diversity of staple food crops will be purchased, this will lead to the farmers being encouraged to grow diversity of food crops in mixed farming systems.

Nutrition schemes need not be just one or two time procurement. They should continue through the year for milk, milk products, vegetables, fruits and eggs. At the time of two main harvests there will be heavy procurement. But smaller procurements will continue throughout the year through the agency of a government procurement representative in the village. This can be a self-help group of women working at a low margin for the benefit of the entire village.

This will help ensure good quality and high nutrition food for nutrition schemes and the public distribution system. Farmers are likely to be more conscious of food safety and quality while meeting the needs of their own village. Farmers, particularly small farmers, will be saved the bother to rush to *mandis* immediately after harvesting. Some cash they receive right in the village will enable farmers to sell their remaining crop in a more relaxed way.

Storages will be created in the village with government help. There will be storage also for any sudden need or emergency. This arrangement is in accordance with the concept of lowering food miles or the concept that food consumption should be close to food production whenever possible. Higher costs of centralized storage will be avoided in this scheme.

This will lead to several food processing activities starting within the village. This can lead the wider shift to village-level processing of food and other crops (such as cotton) much along Gandhian lines.

Besides being good for the village, it will reduce the costs of the government. They will not have to arrange to transport food to the village.

As far as the remaining crop is concerned, some of this can be purchased later by the government for meeting urban and buffer stock needs. Some can be sold elsewhere. In case of bumper crop, the government can purchase some food to send it free to famine affected parts of the world.

The concepts of regional balance in farm development, prioritization of mixed farming systems for meeting local staple food needs, avoiding monocultures, self-reliance of rural communities and eco-friendly low-cost farming are all integral to this thinking of reforms in the procurement sector.

9.2 Procure More Millets, Pulses, Oilseeds

There should be more encouragement to increasing production of pulses, oilseeds and millets. This will be good for nutrition and health of people, good for farm ecology and good for the self-reliance of the country as well as its rural communities.

One of the most disturbing aspects of the farm and food scene in India has been the growing dependence on imported edible oils which now meet the bulk of our requirement. Some of this is suspected to be hazardous GM (genetically modified) oil even though import of GM food products is not allowed. There is also use of domestic GM oil, based on cottonseed oil from Bt cotton. Then there is the high use of unhealthy hydrogenated oil, including import component. Since edible oils are an integral part of most cooked food we eat, our entire food system has become unhealthy, leading to serious diseases.

Hence, we should give high priority to increasing production of traditional healthy oilseeds like groundnut, mustard, coconut and sesame seeds (til). These are well-suited to our nutrition and agro-ecological needs. Procurement at fair price should be increased significantly. Village-level processing of oilseeds should be encouraged. The resulting oilcakes should be saved for our own farm animals instead of being exported. All GM oils sold as edible oils should be declared non-edible oils and phased out in such a way as to avoid any sudden disruption of any livelihoods.

Pulses and legume crops are valuable as staple source of protein in India. These crops are invaluable for maintaining soil health due to their nitrogen fixing abilities. Their presence in mixed cropping systems and rotations is invaluable for soil health. Their production increase should be encouraged, particularly their niche role in mixed systems and rotations, by procuring more at a fair price and in other ways. Their village-level processing should be encouraged to generate more livelihoods.

Millets have been neglected crops for a long time now. Yet these are invaluable for their nutrition role as well as their value in certain agro-ecological conditions in vast parts of our country. Their mixed farming costs very little but provides high nutrition. In adivasi, hilly and desert areas, millet crops are important. The rich traditional knowledge regarding these crops needs to be protected. These should be encouraged by including them in the public distribution system in a significant way.

Encouragement of pulses, millets and oilseeds will be good not just for areas considered less developed but they should be part of the plans to rehabilitate the disrupted ecology and soil health of green revolution areas. In Punjab, the encouragement of these crops by paying better price and procuring more can be an important part of overall efforts to improve agro-ecology.

Overall, the greater encouragement of millets, pulses and traditional oilseeds, because of their great diversity, will contribute much to improving and increasing bio-diversity.

9.3 Why MSP is Not Just a Budget Issue?

The issue of minimum support price or MSP for various crops grown by farmers has seldom attracted the kind of intense debate as in recent times. There is wide agreement that the government should provide MSP for various crops, as this helps to ensure and stabilize a fair price for farmers. However, differences crop up once we go into details like to what extent the government should make available resources for this, how MSP should be calculated, how it should be administered and whether and what kind of legality should be given to this.

The other related responsibility the government has to ensure is food availability at affordable prices, which in real life means making available highly subsidized food to a large number of households. The constraint the government has to keep in mind relates to the extent of subsidy it can afford to provide to the food and farming sector.

One way in which the demand for a legal guarantee for MSP can be realized is by making available so much resources that all the crops for which MSP has been announced (23 leading crops excluding vegetable, fruits, spices) can be purchased by the government.

In other words, we have to multiply estimates of production of crops by MSP of each crop. This comes to around Rs 1.1 million crores or Rs11 lakh crores. Fom this we have to deduct the amount farmers will retain for self-consumption and sharing with relatives. This will reduce the financial burden from Rs 11 lakh crores to about Rs 8 lakh crores.

The government is already spending around Rs 2.7

lakh crores on MSP purchase. So, the actual increase may be around Rs 5.3 lakh crores. If the existing system of sugarcane purchase mostly at private and cooperative levels remains, then the financial implication decreases to around Rs 4.3 lakh crores. Since all the complaints relating to sugarcane purchase by factories will remain, it is better to include sugarcane and let the financial implication remain at Rs 5.3 lakh crores.

The next question is how much the government can earn by selling this huge amount of crops (mostly food crops but also non-food crops like cotton and jute). This is more difficult to estimate as this depends on year-to-year fluctuations of domestic and export price. As the main demand of the government has to be to end hunger and malnutrition, it cannot operate in terms of maximizing gains. Still, if it is estimated that of the Rs 8 lakhs it spends, it can earn about half from sales, then the total burden is Rs 4 lakh crores.

Compared to the existing burden of Rs 2.7 lakh crores, the additional amount is of Rs 1.3 lakh crores which should be manageable. However, this will increase with every increase in MSP. What is more, the main procurement agency already has huge debts. So, the government may be in no mood to increase this financial burden.

Moreover, to the economic costs calculated above should be added the costs relating to infrastructure, storage, salaries and transport (and at the level of practical reality, inefficiency and corruption of most government systems). Hence, economic costs can go up quite a lot. There is the additional question of whether MSP will remain restricted to 23 crops. Demands for MSP for onion, potato, other major vegetables and fruits and spices will be made, particularly when these are important for nutrition programmes.

There are more issues. If a high MSP is assured for a certain crop using chemical fertilizers and excessive water and also for growing it as a monoculture instead of soil protecting mixed farming systems, where will be the incentive to reduce these inputs and costs since MSP will be higher than all these avoidable costs. This is where the dangers of MSP systems which ignore ecological factors come in.

It is possible to create elaborate and expensive MSP based farming systems which may give temporary profits to both relatively well-to-do farmers and agribusiness companies. But with increasing loss of soil health, destruction of natural pollinators, excessive extraction of water and more reliance on monocultures to the exclusion of protective mixed farming and rotations, these systems will begin to collapse after some years. In times of climate change, the dangers of farmers losing heavily in these high external input and high cash cost systems is anyway high. What we need are ecologically protective, low cash cost, low external input and higher self-reliance farming systems.

This is why MSP is not just a budget issue. There is need to look at it in a holistic setting, integrating ecological, economic and other aspects. The government should embark on a huge and well-planned programme with the participation of farmers, based on self-reliant, ecologically protective farming and keeping external costs to a minimum.

Present-day landless households should be given small plots of land or at least kitchen gardens so that all become participants in this effort. When farming costs become much lower and the food produce is healthy, it becomes much easier to ensure all the three objectives -- fair return for farmers, healthy food for all and protection of environment and sustainable livelihood. The finances of such an overall low-cost system will be much easier to manage.

Big Myths of Development Discourse

The economics is untrue which ignores or disregards moral values. The extension of the law of non-violence in the domain of economics means nothing less than introduction of moral values as a factor to be considered in regulating international commerce.

What we seek to do is substitute false and non-human economics by true and human. Not killing competition but life giving cooperation is the law of human being

—Mahatma Gandhi

10.1 Farmer Numbers Must Inevitably Decline?

One of the most widely prevalent beliefs of development discourse is that the number and share of farmers and farmer households in total population must inevitably decline in the course of progress. This is said to be based on historical experience and the fact that technological change and rising productivity make it possible to produce necessary food and raw materials by a much smaller number of persons.

Another argument is that with increase in income, a lesser share is required for food. Based on this and related arguments, a number of experts present estimates of how a huge number of farmers have to shift to other work in a given number of years in India and other similarly placed countries. This is regarded as inevitable and a sign of progress.

This view is so widely prevalent that not just the ruling establishment but even those who claim to be working with the peasantry often share this view even if they don't articulate it openly.

It is important to question this belief and to present an alternative view of development. This is not just an academic debate. Rather it is a basic question of ensuring adequate sustainable livelihoods and protecting environment in difficult times.

The prevailing development discourse is influenced heavily by the experiences of colonial times. Then a large number of persons of present day developed countries could migrate to vast territories colonized by them or lived off the plunder of colonization. But in present times, we cannot so easily talk of people displaced from agriculture finding satisfactory and creative livelihoods elsewhere.

So, rather than thinking of people being uprooted from farming and related activities, we must think instead about people retaining their roots while seeking a diversification of livelihoods in villages, neighboring areas and even in a city. Thus, if there is a household of six members or an extended family (close relatives) of 12 to 15, they retain their base in a village and at the same time reach out for opportunities elsewhere in keeping with their skills, aptitude and education. So a farmer family is also able to access other opportunities from this basic rural base.

To facilitate this, a different development model is needed in which creative, mixed, low-cost and ecologically protective farming is practiced by small farmers. At the same time a lot of small and cottage industries exist in rural and semi-rural areas to produce a lot of other goods which can be made in small, local units. Processing of food as well as non-food crops in particular is encouraged at local rural level. At the same time health and education is improved significantly in rural areas and local jobs are available to a great extent.

Landless rural households are also provided some farmland to the extent possible or else are involved in greening of wasteland in various creative projects. This will offer sustainable livelihoods on the basis of non-timber forest produce and protection of forests. This work, combined with small patches of food crops wherever possible, will give the landless a firm identity and roots in rural life. By helping landless rural workers to become small farmers, the number of farmers goes up significantly instead of decreasing.

This framework of development provides excellent opportunities also to harness the creativity of rural population for checking climate change and related environmental problems.

10.2 Progress is Not Migration

One of the most persistent beliefs in development discourse is that progress inevitably involves shift from rural to urban areas. This is largely rooted in the historical industrial path of progress. But there are a number of important reasons why the past models of development which have brought us to the brink of a survival crisis should be challenged.

Faced with the serious challenge of climate change and related environmental problems, we need different ways of living and thinking. Challenging such well entrenched myths and moving towards doing things differently is an important part of the solution.

There is wide agreement that checking climate change has to be a major priority. While much can be done to reduce GHG emissions in urban areas as well, on the whole the possibilities of large-scale actions for checking climate change are more in rural areas. Whether we think of increasing the organic content of soil or increasing green cover, there are many more possibilities in rural settings. There are also more prospects of integrating this well with a large number of creative livelihoods.

A related part of the myth is that huge amounts of food can be produced in large mechanized monoculture plantations and that existence of rural communities is not integral to meeting food needs. Again, the challenge of climate change brings new emphasis to the importance of promoting vibrant rural communities. The kind of farming needed to arrest climate change – involving protecting and increasing organic matter in soil, protecting and increasing overall green cover, involving mixed farming of several kinds – is not possible in mechanized monoculture. It needs communities of small farmers and family farmers who are most suitable for this highly creative and skilled work. This is also useful for the availability of safe and healthy food as well as secure, sustainable livelihoods.

Similarly, food processing is most healthy, most linked to livelihood protection, most linked to environment protection and least wasteful when it takes place at the level of rural communities. Further, many other kinds of needs can also be met in cottage and small-scale units in rural areas in more environment-friendly ways.

In addition, it is possible for rural households to retain their base in villages while availing of additional opportunities in urban areas. This will forge a supportive, complementing relationship instead of one that involves uprooting, displacement or permanently shifting or moving away.

It should be possible to avoid the dense concentration of population in a few mega cities which is leading to intolerable levels of pollution and other problems. It is also possible to improve things within the existing mega cities in several creative ways. Mega cities may also have some advantages which should be built on. At the same time, it is good to create conditions of more dispersed activity and population rather than concentrated and centralized ones.

Environment Protection and Climate Change

Few of us realise the havoc that modern agricultural practices are wreaking on our countryside. Farmers have forgotten the habits that supported a wide variety of wildlife and countless varieties of wild plants, flowers and trees that are essential for profitable and sustainable agriculture. What is happening in farming today is that the agriculture technology is acting in isolation, treating organisms in isolation, which leads to a disturbance of the natural system of checks and balances. It should be a sensitive balance of organisms in nature that should be allowed to spread. Few people realize today that there is a certain symbiosis between the various elements of nature like between flowers and pollen, soil and organisms. The role of the ecological balance in managing habitat has to grow.

—GR Iyengar
Organic farmer of India

11.1 Ecologically Protective Farming

While the social benefits of ecologically protective, organic and/or natural farming are so obvious, it is sometimes said that in economic terms this may not be so beneficial for farmers. This thinking becomes a big hurdle in the spread of ecologically protective farming. The advocates of ecologically protective and low external input farming give several reasons to argue why and how this can also be a wiser option in terms of economic benefits and these economic benefits are likely to increase even more in future years.

Ultimately, what matters for a farmer's income in economic terms is not total cash receipt but the net income – sales receipts minus costs. If costs can be reduced drastically, then net income will go up significantly even if all other aspects remain the same. In ecologically protective, organic/natural farming, the costs of market purchased inputs can decrease greatly. It is true that in some forms of organic farming costs of organic certification can be high. But such expensive certification must be rejected by India and most other developing countries. Instead, we can have community based certification and the trust achieved by the adoption of organic farming in an entire village or region.

The mixed farming systems practised in ecologically protective farming make it possible to harvest small crops at different times of the year so that some cash earnings come in throughout the year. The dependence on one or two big harvests a year in monoculture farming will go.

Thirdly, it is possible to tap the market for healthy foods and obtain a somewhat higher price for the products of ecologically protective agriculture. In its procurement, the government should agree to give a higher price for the products of ecologically protective farming. In the export market also it is increasingly likely that a better price and more acceptance will exist for GM-free organic products. The government should ensure that the benefits of this better price reach farmers.

With much lower costs and no need to incur debts for expensive external inputs, the risks and indebtedness of farmers will plunge.

Are farmers and farming communities looking for only immediate gains? Or are they also considering the options before future generations? When we give adequate consideration to future, then we have to look at the sustainability of the farming system as well as the basic resources of soil and health. When we look at the economics of future, then ecologically protective ways have much better economic prospects for farming communities.

Lastly, in times of climate change, the value of ecologically protective farming increases greatly. This is because it can protect and increase organic matter in soil and increase the overall greenery. Hence, a strong case exists for regular transfer of funds from an international fund for checking climate change to those rural communities which practice organic/natural farming.

Farmer organizations need to respond to this challenge and accept the move towards ecologically protective agriculture. The government should understand this at the right time and formulate policies accordingly. Government help and subsidies can help farmers in the initial stage of moving towards ecologically protective agriculture.

11.2 Organic Farmers Need Support

There is worldwide realization that food system is becoming less safe and healthy. This is to a large extent because of the use of excessive chemical fertilizers, pesticides and herbicides. Some of the inputs have been found to be so poisonous and harmful that it is distressing their use in food and farming systems ever got authorized.

After World War II ended, some of the weapon factories found a new diversion in chemical fertilizers and chemical pesticides. This is how a highly harmful trend started in the food and farming system. The giant corporations, instead of taking remedial actions, are trying to dominate the world food system. They are moving in the direction of more hazards such as GM foods. A shift is taking place from naturally grown foods towards industrial foods grown with a fearful cocktail of industrial chemicals.

The aim to reap super profits is sought to be covered up with the help of peddler 'experts'. If these experts have their way, hardly any natural, healthy, wholesome food will be left in a dystopian future.

To counter this, we need small farmer-based farming using eco-friendly, organic methods to produce safe and healthy food. In countries like India, there is no room for expensive certification procedures. We need low-cost and very self-reliant organic farming based on making the best use of local resources.

While it is necessary to give up chemical fertilizers and pesticides, it is equally important to emphasize that careful nurturing of farms is needed, all the while learning from nature and natural processes.

As a new generation of farmers has grown up which has seen only chemical-intensive farming, sustained organic farming campaigns are needed. Even in areas where chemical-intensive farming has not spread much, it is being promoted as a model of progress. Campaigns to protect diversity of traditional seeds are needed as they are certainly more important from the point of view of organic farming.

In addition, efforts to link organic farmers with consumers in cities are also needed. Certain identified villages of organic farmers can be linked to certain urban colonies without any middlemen or curbs. Cottage scale food processing can add valuc to urganic food crops.

Sahbhagi Vikash Abhiyan in Odisha has encouraged organic farmers in various ways while setting up cottage scale rural food processing units to add value. Save the Seeds Movement in Uttarakhand has worked for several years for saving traditional seeds and mixed farming systems. Alliance for Sustainable and Holistic Agriculture or ASHA has consistently protected and promoted organic farming and advanced the common interests and concerns of its members.

A programme which has tried to combine these various efforts in several states of India is called *Bhoomi Ka*. Supported by Welthungerhilfe and involving numerous social and environmental activists, this has reached out to many farmers for promoting organic farming. Training is also organised. When such initiatives progress, community and/or farmer producer groups are formed to take forward the work. At the same time, efforts are made to forge links with consumers in cities and to facilitate the inter-action of farmers and consumers. Safe and healthy food issues are introduced in educational work. Campaigns for safe food contribute to improving the market prospects of organic farmers.

While all such efforts are welcome, their strength is much less compared to the powerful big business interests. Hence, much bigger campaigns are needed to take organic farming forward in highly self-reliant and very low-cost ways.

If such campaigns can convince governments to be more supportive, then a substantial share of the organic food crops grown in a village can be purchased by the government at a fair price for allocation to nutrition programmes and ration shops of the same village.

11.3 Let Kitchen Gardens Bloom

While issues relating to farmers are discussed widely, we need to also take up what confronts farmer households. That the farmers need to be provided at least small plots of cultivation land had a lot of acceptance till the not-too-distant past. Around this acceptance policies were framed; legislations were enacted and special drives for providing land to the landless were launched. It is a measure of the changes that have taken place in recent times that hardly anyone in the Union Government and most state governments even talks about this now.

Even in these adverse conditions, it is important to keep alive the idea of land reforms and land for the landless. A beginning can perhaps be made by promoting the idea of kitchen gardens for landless households. This means that all landless households should have secure homestead rights in the village. Attached to this should be the right to cultivate a little land near their homes and hamlets and make use of the waste kitchen water and compostable wastes. These kitchen gardens can grow a diversity of foods with emphasis on nutritious green leafy vegetables. Organic methods should be used for this. Purchase of industrial inputs should be avoided as much as possible. The government can help by giving a small grant per kitchen garden and prizes for the most creative such efforts in a panchayat. Poultry and animal husbandry can be encouraged simultaneously.

Of course, this concept will depend on housing, location of hamlet of landless households and other local factors. A highly decentralized, local-specific approach is needed. Many creative possibilities will emerge in the process of consultations and implementation.

Needless to add, this is envisaged as a limited aspect of land rights. The possibilities of wider land reforms, including the concept of a minimum land holding, remain open.

Similarly, kitchen garden is relevant for other rural poor households also. In fact, this is relevant even for urban poor households. Space is a limiting constraint in an urban settlement. But, as they say, where there is a will there is a way. Sometimes productive and creative use can be made even of small patches of land or terraces. This keeps the urban migrant in touch with plants and greenery. This itself is a contribution in addition to some availability of nutritious vegetables.

11.4 Urban Gardening

Gardening is a popular hobby in Indian cities. Although in a majority of households there is hardly any space for gardening, the green urge and creativity of many people find an outlet somehow, even if this is confined to a few earthen pots. The sheer joy of plucking home-grown coriander or mint leaves, a green chilly or two, even an occasional brinjal can cheer up a household.

Basil (Tulsi) is the most common (and most useful) plant for urban households in India. Creepers offer a way of growing useful vegetables and beautiful flowers even in the absence of open space. Terrace gardens open up many creative possibilities. There are fortunate households which have a proper garden.

This instinctive creativity of urban people needs to be tapped in ways so that it becomes something much more than a hobby. It can contribute in more meaningful ways to a safer and healthier food system. In the absence of such an understanding, this creativity can play only a restrictive role. Sometimes this becomes harmful. Thus, lacking a wider perspective, people fall into the trap of using excessive chemical fertilizers and other harmful inputs to obtain quick initial growth of plant or obtain a shining product.

This is harmful for the soil, micro-organisms, beneficial insects like butterflies and bees, birds, animals as well as human beings. Food obtained in this way is neither healthy nor safe. The purpose of gardening is largely defeated if such chemical intensive methods are used.

Many in urban areas seek the help of gardeners. The traditional 'maali' is a useful person and is well-informed about plants. But many gardeners try to make you spend on chemical fertilizers and pesticides or on seeds which respond well only when fed by these expensive and harmful inputs.

This is the reason why the admirable and potentially very useful instincts of urban people for gardening are at present not leading to useful social and ecological impacts. It may well be leading to a lot of harm to health and ecology.

We need a campaign to make urban gardening eco-friendly and safer. Such a campaign can help ensure that the instinctive creativity of millions of urban gardeners leads to beneficial results. This will involve better consciousness regarding organic food, leading to more demand for safe and healthy food.

The more people realize the importance of safe and healthy food for their overall well-being, the more inclined they will be towards organic gardening cities. This includes composting of biodegradable waste. Once this is accepted as important, the trend towards waste-segregation at source and decentralized composting units within housing colonies will get a big boost.

This should not be confined to middle- and upper-class colonies. It should spread to hutments and slums as well where waste water from kitchens can be used for kitchen gardens. These efforts can be useful to grow vegetables.

Bhoomi Ka has contributed much to these highly desirable objectives and activities in several cities of India. Supported by WHH (Welthungerhilfe), this programme has included trainings in organic farming, events promoting cooking of organic and healthy food, organization of fairs and festivals of healthy food, educational work on safe food, encouraging interaction of urban people with organic farmers and related activities. Although the Covid-related limitations diminished some of these activities, it was used to continue some of the interactions and trainings. More such campaigns and trainings are needed. Gardeners can also be involved.

11.5 Cuba's Hope for Farmers

Cuba's progress in agriculture over the last 25 years or so have given a new hope to farmers and environmentalists all over the world. Cuba has managed to increase food production in adverse conditions by relying largely on eco-friendly methods. At the same time, it has reduced significantly the use of chemical fertilizers and pesticides.

The Cuban success story is attributed not just to eco-friendly methods but also to the equality of its farm and land structure. There is cooperation among small peasants and scientists working in cooperation with people. The Cuban model is a convincing alternative to the corporatization of agriculture.

In the early 1990s, Cuban agriculture and food system faced a big crisis as the import of food and fertilizers from its most friendly country, on which it was heavily dependent, collapsed with the disintegration of the Soviet Union.

While imports and help fell in adverse conditions, pressures from a hostile US increased in various ways. There were also crippling economic sanctions. Pushed from all sides and facing a big decline in food production, Cuba planned to achieve self-reliance in food by using sustainable and self-reliant methods. Local resources were used instead of relying on imports. This led to a successful and sustained application of the agro-ecology approach.

Agro-ecology has been much discussed since the 1970s. Several farmer and environmental groups around the world have implemented it with encouraging results. In Cuba, for the first time, it was adopted as a national policy. Its implementation has been sustained and is still continuing.

Agro-ecology is based on learning from nature, and incorporating nature's ways into farming and food production. This includes essential aspects of organic farming. It adds to it a more social (as compared to a merely technical) approach, including learning from indigenous knowledge.

The input and technology changes included more reliance on worm humus, poultry manure and bio-fertilizers instead of chemical fertilizers. This was supported by recycling of nutrients, better and more integration of crops and animals, and intercropping. Soil conservation received better attention. Many centers were set up to promote bio-control agents and other alternatives to chemical pesticides. Cases of pesticide poisoning started dropping rapidly. Favourable laws were passed for eco-friendly farming. Farmers and their cooperatives were encouraged to follow this eco-friendly path. These changes progressed both at the level of official policy as well as a movement of farmers and their organizations.

This approach started giving impressive results within six years or so. The results have been maintained since then. By 2007, food production had not just recovered but grown significantly compared to pre-disruption levels. In the 1996-97 season, Cuba recorded its then highest production levels for 10 out of 13 basic food crops.

While similar success of increasing production while reducing agro-chemicals has also been achieved in smaller areas of several countries, Cuba provides the foremost example of initiating this at a national level for a long period.

Agro-ecology is also more labour intensive and creative. Hence more people get an opportunity to be engaged in creative livelihoods. For those so inclined, agro-ecology is a constant source of creative learning and experimentation.

For children agro-ecology can be a good and creative source of science and farming education and nature-learning. This approach also helps farmers to cut down on expenses of costly agro-chemicals.

In the course of this progress, Cuban farmers and scientists realized they have much to learn from their past. As Peter Rosset, who has studied Cuban agriculture extensively, has written, 'In almost every case they said they had remembered the old techniques – like intercropping and manure – that their parents and grandparents had used before the advent of modern chemicals, simultaneously incorporating bio-pesticides and bio-fertilizers into their production practices.'

11.6 Farming and Climate Change

To beat climate change, all sectors must contribute to a reduction of greenhouse gas emissions. The extremely important contribution the food and agriculture sector can make was underestimated initially. More and more research now indicates that this sector's role can be extremely important. If all the potential of this sector is more or less fully tapped, this can perhaps make the most important contribution in checking climate change.

In a study titled *The Great Climate Robbery*, GRAIN, a reputed international organization working on small farmers and sustainable farming, has written: The expansion of unsustainable agricultural practices over the past century has led to the destruction of between 30 percent and 75 percent of the organic matter on arable lands, and 50 percent of the organic matter on pastures and prairies. This massive loss of organic matter is responsible for between 25 percent and 40 percent of the current excess carbon dioxide in the earth's atmosphere.

On the plus side, this study points out that this damage can be undone substantially 'simply by restoring the practices small farmers have been engaging in for generations. If the right policies and incentives were in place worldwide, soil organic matter contents could be restored to pre-industrial agriculture levels within a period of 50 years.... This would offset between 24 and 30 percent of all current global greenhouse gas emissions.'

This study emphasizes that farmers can maintain their present yields while giving up chemical fertilizers by using agro-ecology. This is confirmed by the International Assessment of Agricultural Knowledge, Science and Technology for Development (IAASTD). The International Panel for Climate Change has estimated that for every 100 kg of nitrogen fertilizer applied in the soil, one kg ends up in the atmosphere as nitrous oxide, a gas that is 300 times more potent than carbon dioxide as a greenhouse gas and is the world's most significant ozone depleting substance.

The GRAIN study also pointed out that supply of natural gas for nitrogen fertilser may now rely more on fracked wells, which leak about 50 percent more methane gas compared to conventional natural gas wells. Methane is 25 times more potent than carbon dioxide as a greenhouse gas. So the prospect of reducing GHG emissions just by shifting to agro-ecology from chemical fertilisers is immense. But there are so many other aspects of changing food and agriculture system to reduce GHG emissions.

There can be a big reduction of GHG emissions by ensuring food consumption close to food production and by reducing miles travelled by food and by cutting down on wasteful processing and packaging. A huge reduction of chemical pesticides and herbicides has been demanded time and again for so many other reasons including health and safety. This will also help significantly reduce GHG emissions.

GHG emissions are known to be very high in the big plantations and livestock operations taken up by giant agro-business corporations. They can be reduced by meeting food needs from other sources and redistributing the huge land holdings of these big operators among landless and near landless peasants and farm workers.

There are numerous creative ways of reducing GHG emissions in the food and farming system. Traditional farming methods had been able to maintain and enhance soil organic matter for several centuries. Industrial extractive farming systems have depleted soil organic matter rapidly.

11.7 Climate Change and Farmers' Welfare

Climate change is one of the most critical problems of our times. Its disrupting impacts on farming and related activities is being felt by farmers, pastorals and others in the form of highly erratic and extreme weather as well as rise in the intensity and frequency of various disasters.

Two questions arise: How can farmers contribute majorly to reducing greenhouse gas emissions? How can they adapt well to climate change to minimize damage and distress?

It is important to plan the response to climate change in such a way that this is well-integrated with improved welfare and livelihoods of farmers. This needs to be emphasized as some business interests are trying to emerge as leaders of climate change. They are trying to impose a highly distorted agenda of farm sector response to climate change to advance their own interests.

Firstly, it is increasingly realized that the kind of farming needed to check climate change can be done only by small farmers. We need farming which can reduce fossil fuels greatly (which means a massive reduction in chemical fertilizers, pesticides, excessive mechanization) and enhance organic content of soil, more particularly by adopting mixed cropping systems and integrating trees, animal husbandry and poultry with farming. This is possible when skilled small farmers devote care and creativity to soil and crops. This role cannot be performed by highly mechanized, fossil fuel guzzling plantations of big players.

Secondly, enhancing and improving the organic content of soil is important to arrest climate change. This is also important for small and medium farmers to improve their yields (without having to purchase expensive inputs) in sustainable, self-reliant ways and keeping costs at low levels.

Thirdly, banning GM crops is good for farmers due to high risks of GM technology for farming, environment and safe food. At the same time, the highly centralized, big business dominated farming that GM technology brings is difficult to reconcile with what is needed to check climate change. A highly decentralized system in which farmers are self-reliant and can quickly respond to new situations is much better.

Last but not the least, there are good possibilities that an international fund for responding to climate change (checking climate change or adjusting to it, mitigation and adaptation) can be created. This will make regular payments to rural communities and farmers whose farming and related practices contribute significantly to battling climate change and reducing the distress caused by it.

11.8 Ecologically Protective Methods

Recently, Sant Seechewal, an award winning eco-activist of Punjab, visited protesting farmers at Delhi border with a truckload of healthy food. The message he brought was more precious — he called upon them to shift to natural farming and mutually cooperative farming in order to find more reliable and sustainable solutions to their problems.

Some well-intentioned persons who agree with the wisdom of this message have raised questions regarding how to give practical expression to this message in such a way that natural or organic or ecologically protective farming can spread in a big way.

We must accept there are problems as over one or two generations of farmers have become used to the ecologically disrupting green revolution farming. Then there are forces which use environment as a garb to push their narrow agenda.

There were reports of a company pushing a solar energy project in a tribal village which disrupted and displaced their traditional livelihoods which were in keeping with environment protection. The company sold it as a project of renewable energy which will check climate change. It ignored the disruption of communities leading ecologically sound life which can never be justified. Solar energy is certainly needed but it should not disrupt communities.

Such problems can become much wider if hydro projects involving a lot of displacement and ecological destruction are pushed as projects which reduce GHG emissions. This trend will be harmful. There are signs of this increasing.

On the other hand, a genuinely GHG emission reducing technology like Mangal Turbine, an invention by farmer scientist Mangal Singh, can greatly reduce diesel consumption in villages. But it has been neglected badly by the government despite appeals from eminent persons.

The case for ecologically protective farming has been strengthened due to their enormous benefits vis-à-vis climate change. Properly guided eco-friendly farming can greatly increase organic content of soil and can push up greenery. With more self-reliance and decentralization as well as reduced costs, this can adapt much better to climate change.

Big business trying to dominate global food and farming

system proclaim false advantages of GM crops. They get media attention while the reality is that the already strong case for banning GM crops has strengthened further due to climate change related factors.

The real challenge is to bring in policies which will promote eco-friendly farming by small and medium farmers, including the landless. There are short-term difficulties in this but the government should sort these out instead of creating problems.

11.9 Alternative Food and Farming Systems

The food and farming system at the world level is getting increasingly dominated by powerful corporate interests. The motives driving them is maximizing profits and dominance. In the process the system has been moving away from the objectives of producing safe and adequate healthy food on sustainable basis while ensuring creative and satisfactory livelihoods. In these difficult conditions several groups and individuals are steadfastly working for creating an alternative food and farming system. It is useful to look at some of these efforts and their vision.

Several UK farming, consumer, organic, animal welfare, environmental and Third World groups formed the Sustainable Agriculture, Food and Environment (SAFE) alliance. The SAFE Alliance tried to define the requirements of a good agricultural system as:

- An agriculture that is supportive of rural communities, that halts the decline in full-time farm employment and provides a stable livelihood for farmers and farm workers;

- An agriculture that does not jeopardize the health of those who work or live on the land or the consumer through the use of polluting or toxic production methods;
- An agriculture that is capable of flexible response to national food and nutrition goals designed to improve public health;
- An agriculture that produces affordable food, of high nutritional quality and that minimizes chemical and microbiological contaminants;
- An agriculture that does not lead to the reduction of soil fertility, that minimizes reliance on non-renewable resources and that is sustainable;
- An agriculture that both conserves and enhances the countryside, not only in its visual aspect but also in terms of its resources and wildlife;
- An agriculture that respects the welfare needs of farm animals;
- An agriculture that does not threaten the development and maintenance of food security and sustainable agriculture in other countries, especially those in the Third World.

A good food and agricultural system is one which makes available satisfactory livelihood to all members of the farming community (including landless workers and sharecroppers or tenants) and wholesome, nutritious food to all people in a sustainable way. It ensures welfare of farm animals and protects bio-diversity and environment with emphasis on soil, water and pollinators.

Unfortunately, the world today is far away from such a system. There is a lot of economic tension and uncertainty among farmers not only in developing countries but also in some of the richest countries. A significant share of the farming community is landless (or near landless) and it is deprived of a fair share of the farm income. Many landholders are themselves in danger of losing control over their land.

Again, even in the richest countries, care of soil is badly neglected. The machines that have taken over most work can produce more food but cannot protect soil for future generations. As more and more skilled peasants are driven away from agriculture, it becomes more and more unlikely that enough people will be available not just to produce food but to protect land. Farm animals and other forms of life are treated ruthlessly.

Poverty and inequalities deny adequate food to a large number of people (probably nearly one billion). Even those with purchasing power find it increasingly difficult to get wholesome, nutritious food due to the domination in markets of what is heavily treated by chemicals.

So, the basic priorities of improving the farm and agriculture system should be:

- Empower those who work on farmland to maintain their close links with land.
- Support them to get an adequate livelihood from cultivating the land and protecting its soil and water.
- Establish harmony between the welfare of farm animals and economic returns of farming. In other words, make productive use of farm animals to bring economic

returns without being cruel to them.

- Establish direct links between farmers and consumers so that the latter can get good quality food. Farmers can secure a fair price in return. Monitor trade, processing and middlemen interests carefully to ensure that interests of farmers and consumers are not violated. Role of small traders is often fine but that of big business has to be checked.

Unfortunately, almost all these concerns are being neglected. The existing distortions are getting worse due to the domination of quick profits seeking big agribusiness in policy matters. The longer-term and more significant interests of ordinary farmers and consumers are ignored. A lot of confusion arises from treating agriculture much like an industry. The fallacy of this view has been very aptly exposed by Wendell Berry, farmer-philosopher from the US, 'The farmer differs from the industrialist in that the farmer is necessarily a nurturer, a preserver of the health of creatures. The economy of industry is, typically, extractive. It takes, makes, uses, and discards, it progresses, that is from exhaustion to pollution. Agriculture, on the other hand, rightly belongs to a replenishing economy, which takes, makes, uses, and returns - it involves the return to the source, not just of fertility or of so-called wastes, but also of care and affection.'

Arguing why this basic understanding of agriculture is so missed these days Berry writes, The 'free market' – the unbridled play of economic forces – is bad for agriculture because it is unable to assign a value to things that are necessary to agriculture. It gives a value to agricultural products, but it cannot give a value to the sources of those products in the topsoil, the ecosystem, the farm, the farm family or the farm community. Indeed, people who look at farming from the standpoint of the 'free market' do not understand the relation of product to source. They believe that the relation is merely mechanical because they believe that agriculture is or can be an industry. And the 'free market' is helpless to suggest otherwise.

There are thus very strong reasons why several economists, allied experts and politicians advised by them are unlikely to appreciate the true nature of agricultural work. This explains why governments are so reluctant to implement the genuinely needed agricultural reforms. Government policy and business interests, including experts who function as fronts of business interests, distort the meaning of the word reform and actually increase distortions. Hence farmers in many parts of world have become wary and skeptical about experts who dominate the farming discourse.

11.10 Protecting Land from Predatory Capitalism

India has over 16 percent of the world's population and 2 percent of the world's land. The livelihoods of nearly two thirds of India's population are linked to farmlands, village commons and forests. Given the scarcity of land as well as the extent of livelihoods linked to it, it is of the greatest importance to plan land use in such a way that the base of sustainable livelihoods is protected. The importance of this task has increased immensely due to climate change. Sustainable livelihoods based on greenery are more beneficial for reducing greenhouse gas (GHG) emissions compared to a situation where these livelihoods are uprooted.

However, just when the importance of protecting 'green livelihoods' and their base (particularly farmland and forests) is the greatest, tragically the assault on agricultural land, commons and forests is the greatest. As the path of capitalist development spawns increasing inequalities, and gets more forcefully linked to the forces of globalisation, the nature of such growth and linkages creates conditions of a relentless assault on sustainable livelihoods.

To make this clearer, we may classify the various factors due to which the base of sustainable, land-based livelihoods (mainly agriculture, horticulture, animal husbandry) and mixed farming systems based on a combination of these can be threatened.

1. Even in a reasonably balanced path of development, there will be pressure on some agriculture and forest land due to growing demand for industrial goods, infrastructure and urbanization. However, this can be managed without serious damage if there is a well-thought policy for saving fertile farmland and natural forests. This policy has to be implemented in participation with rural people.
2. The situation gets difficult if the path involves extreme inequalities as in this case there is excessive pressure on production of luxury goods, luxury housing, hotels and resorts.
3. If the development path gives less priority to farmers, shifts terms of trade against agriculture and provides

them little insurance in times of greater uncertainty, then it becames easy for land speculators to uproot farmers.

4. If land speculators and mafias are allowed to flourish in collusion with corrupt officials and politicians, the prospects for excessive land grabbing in the guise of development work goes up greatly.
5. When the national economy is more deeply drawn into the web of globalization, the pressure to meet the demands of global elite increases the pressure on sustainable livelihoods and their base. The global demands for minerals can be particularly huge. There are also pressures for industrial or other goods commanded by globalisation based specialisation for various countries/regions. This often pushes more polluting and displacement-causing activities to poorer countries, bringing super profits to a few but misery to most.

While threats to sustainable livelihoods arising from factor (1) can be managed within reasonable limits, factors (2) to (5) when combined together can increase these threats manifold. They can even become limitless given the pull of speculative forces and global demand. In such a situation, any planning to protect the base of sustainable livelihoods becomes very difficult. Firstly, the global pressures cannot be predicted and secondly, powerful interests of speculators and land grabbers create serious problems for any such planning.

Therefore, any serious effort to challenge the threat to sustainable livelihoods based on farmland, commons and forests should resist factors (2) to (5). If these forces are not weakened, then the assault on sustainable livelihoods will continue to grow. However, government policy at present is not based on any such wider commitment.

Within the framework of the democratic system in India, the government's main concern is not to check the assault, or the extent of the assault, on farmland and forests. It is rather to manage and contain the distress and discontent this is likely to cause among farmers, pastorals, forest-produce gatherers and other sustainable livelihood occupations. In states like West Bengal, one saw how volatile issues like land acquisition led to electoral debacles for well-entrenched ruling coalitions.

Therefore, the entire effort is usually to think of a package of compensation which will satisfy the farmers facing land acquisition. Towards this end, the state governments of Haryana, Gujarat and Uttar Pradesh have come up with their own versions of an ideal package and other states may soon follow. Now attention is more focused on the national-level efforts to provide a 'model' law on land acquisition as well as rehabilitation of displaced people. While various provisions of these laws are hotly debated, without challenging factors (2) to (5) mentioned above, the impact of any legislative measures on reducing the threat to sustainable livelihoods can only be limited.

Here, it is important to bring out the basic difference between two kinds of objectives:

(a) Somehow reduce the discontent and protests against land acquisition without necessarily reducing the extent of land acquisition;

(b) Focus on the need to reduce significantly the assault on farmland, commons and forests and the sustainable livelihoods based on these.

These are two contrasting objectives and should not be confused with one another. The government appears to be mainly concerned with the first. Many senior persons in the government may not even accept the second objective as desirable. In fact, a senior minister said some time back that the ideal development of the country he has in mind is for 85 percent of the people to live in cities (compared to the 30 percent urban population today).

However, for several social and environmental movements, objective (b) is more important. This is from the point of both sustainable livelihoods and environment protection (as well as overall welfare).

- If fertile farmland, commons and forests are protected, then sustainable livelihoods for many, many generations will be assured.
- In a world where food security is increasingly threatened, this will lead to adequate availability of food crops, milk and several nutritious food in forests.
- At a time when bio-diversity is badly threatened, this will contribute to its protection.
- This will help strengthen rural communities which are threatened in many ways and make available a better, more sustainable pattern of life.
- This will help to reduce GHG emissions. The pattern of sustainable development based on

green cover is always better than the pattern of mostly polluting industrial and infrastructure development.

- If the assault on farmland is stopped, the possibilities of land reforms or distribution of farmland among the landless rural poor can increase. To reduce rural poverty, land distribution among the landless can prove effective.
- Large-scale displacement from land is likely to lead to massive unemployment. Capital-intensive industrialisation can provide limited employment to those uprooted from land.

Hence, what needs to be emphasised is the necessity of protecting sustainable livelihoods – fertile farmland, commons and forests (and water sources). Short-term remedial measures or appeasement of affected farmers with compensation is not the answer. The focus should be on challenging and checking the current paradigm of development.

How to achieve this in the face of ganging up of powerful interests? Here are some suggestions for strengthening these struggles and the overall effort for checking the assault on farmland, commons and forests.

- Bring the various struggles to protect the 'good earth' closer so that they contribute to each other's success.
- Mobilize pro-people professional expertise so that well-researched, comprehensive, cost benefit studies can be made for various projects related

to food security, sustainable livelihoods, GHG emissions and bio-diversity.

- Set up state-level and national platforms to take up issues of common interests.
- Link these national initiatives to international organisations working on sustainable development alternatives.
- There should be a well-organized campaign for alternative paradigms of development.

If local to world-level linkages can be made and if the perspectives of food security and sustainable development can be combined effectively, then the prospects of checking the assault on poverty can improve significantly. This effort should include media campaigns, regular dialogue with legislators, political parties, academics and opinion makers as well as public interest litigations.

The Perspective of Land Reforms

In this entire discussion, the perspective of land reforms needs to be brought in. The government has repeatedly gone back on its promises of significant redistribution of farmland. The massive assault on farmland and displacement of people have a very adverse impact on the possibilities of land reforms. When even land-owning farmers are losing their land on a vast scale, who will care to give land to landless peasants?

When land is acquired for various projects, farm workers, tenants, sharecroppers and artisans are often left in the lurch. They lose their livelihoods. They don't have any land ownership papers to claim compensation and other 'benefits'. Although some efforts have been made to partly alienate some of these problems, on the whole assaults on land, commons and forests also harm the poorest landless people in various ways. Several landless or others who got land after years of efforts also lose their fields in the assaults on farmland.

The movements struggling on behalf of the landless and the near landless should widen their horizons as many farmers face the threat of becoming landless.

The Proposal for Minimum Holding

It is in this wider context that the proposal for a law to ensure minimum land holding for all long-term resident rural households acquires significance. Such a law could lay down that all long-term residents of a village will have rights to homestead land and at least an acre of cultivation land. The size of the land holding can differ in hill and plain areas and also in irrigated and desert areas.

Importance of such a law has increased as it can give minimum security not only to landless people but also to others threatened with landlessness. The law can compel the authorities to ensure that some minimum land base of any family is not disturbed.

This will have multiple benefits.

- It will help significantly in poverty alleviation and food security in the context of the poorest families.
- It will help poorest families to explore additional livelihood opportunities including food crop production, animal husbandry and cottage scale crafts.

- It will improve health and hygiene of poorest families as they have space for toilets, bathrooms and dairy or other animals.
- It will strengthen rural communities.
- Several rural households have said that even a small plot of land gives them social dignity.

The proposal for a minimum land holding deserves immediate attention to promote food security and poverty alleviation.

11.11 Farmers Can Save Themselves and the World

Across the world, even small and medium farmers are facing increasing distress. At the same time, the livelihood problems of the rural landless are rising in many contexts, worsening further post Covid.

Given the unending weather uncertainties and extremes, will this livelihood crisis not worsen in the near future? And if farmers are in deep trouble, won't this affect the food security in several ways?

This is why it is vital to plan carefully for a development path which ensures sustainable livelihoods for farmers as well as landless households. At the same time, it must reorient agriculture to provide adequate healthy food and contribute to checking climate change. Fortunately, it is still possible to simultaneously achieve all these objectives. The following plan of action is needed for this.

Farming has to be based on social agro-ecology approach. This implies use of ecologically protective methods on farming which protect soil, conserve water and moisture and protect all farmer-friendly forms of life. This needs to be achieved by minimizing external and ecologically disruptive inputs while optimizing local ecologically protective resources. There should be emphasis on providing more green cover of indigenous plants, trees and grasses. There should be great emphasis on protecting and re-generating pastures and natural mixed forests and saving groves, orchards and pathways of indigenous mixed trees.

Much higher economic resources should be available for farms, pastures and forests. These should reach rural communities directly for ecologically protective, sustainable livelihood activities. In addition, a substantial fund for climate change should be established internationally. The bulk of it should be for rural communities of poorer countries of global south if they are committed to this ecologically protective development path.

This can be used to support farmers who take up ecologically protective farming and to assure basic support in times of adverse weather and disaster.

Attempts should be made to find small plots of farmland for the landless. The landless should also get the most opportunities in greening efforts, including regeneration of degraded pastures, forests and groves. These initiatives can have smaller components of farming and dairying to add to livelihood support.

Food processing should be substantially in the hands of rural communities, led by women and traditional communities involved in this work. This as well as public health, public education, information sectors, crafts and arts plus eco-friendly tourism should get a big boost in rural areas.

The problem is there are powerful forces which not only hinder such progress but impose their narrow agenda, pushing the world in the opposite direction of ecological ruin.

This is where the biggest challenge lies. A democratic and well-informed dialogue can easily identify the path ahead but the dominance of powerful forces hinders this. Hence the task becomes much more difficult. This is where we stand today, at the crossroads of the potential of great improvements which, with help, rural communities can bring, and the catastrophic disruptions which powerful forces seem bent on unleashing.

The Search for Alternatives

A good food and agricultural system is one which makes available satisfactory livelihood to all members of the farming community and wholesome, nutritious food to all people in a sustainable way ensuring welfare of farm animals, protecting the soil and its fertility for future generations.

—Bharat Dogra

12.1 Farming and Food System India Needs

We need to initiate a debate on what alternative system of farming and food the country needs. It is not enough to criticize the existing system. We should be clear about what we actually need.

We have defined Social Agro-Ecology as the meeting point of equality and environment, justice and safety, of livelihood and health. We have argued strongly for a farming and food system based on this. But this applies to the entire world. We need to look in detail at the specific situation in our country.

India is blessed with a diversity of agro-climatic and agro-geographical situations calling for a highly decentralized approach to farm development. So, over-centralization in farming should never have taken place. After the green revolution, this has been harmful for Indian agriculture. It should be given up. A decentralized farming can utilize fully the traditional wisdom in all respects but particularly in the context of diversity of seeds and water/moisture conservation.

Agriculture in India has been characterized by highly uneven development. One aspect of this is regional imbalances. Another is imbalance between main cereals on the one hand and millets, legumes and oilseeds on the other hand. These imbalances should be corrected.

India should strive to obtain self-reliance in all staple foods including oilseeds and edible oils. This self-reliance should be achieved as soon as possible. Import of all unnecessary luxury foods should be avoided.

Imports of food and farm produce which directly harm our farmers should be curbed. Imports of all hazardous foods including GM foods should be banned.

As far as possible, efforts should be made to transform all areas largely self-reliant of meeting their staple food needs of cereals, millets, edible oils, legumes and vegetables.

All regions should try to produce enough of staple foods plus storage for difficult times. All areas should strive to produce some extra food to be donated to fighting hunger. Traditional practices and community kitchens should be promoted.

Ending hunger and malnutrition should be a top priority for the country. To achieve this, top priority should be given to farming and food production. Adequate resources should be allocated to the farm sector. These should directly reach farmers. The tendency of giving subsidies to industrial interests in the name of farming and farmers should be stopped.

Farm and food processing should get maximum encouragement at the rural decentralized level. The entire effort must be led by rural women. The big contribution of women to farming and food processing should be respected. There should be curbs on wasteful and harmful processing which destroy the nutritional value of natural food or introduce harmful substances.

Ecologically, farming practices should be promoted at all levels. India should be made a centre of safe, healthy and highly nutritious food produced by ecologically protective methods. Farmers and villages which excel in ecologically protective farming methods and production of safe foods should get generous rewards. Farmers and villages must be honoured for using methods which protect soil fertility, conserve water, save bio-diversity and produce safe and nutritious staple food.

Huge monocultures should be avoided. As far as possible mixed farming systems which combine the production of several staple foods with animal husbandry and bee-keeping should be followed. Attempts should be made to protect and revive traditional diversity of seeds so that farmers can be self-reliant.

Farm animals should get more attention due to their higher contribution in ecologically protective, organic/natural farming systems. All relations with farm animals, be it cow or earthworm or bee or frog, should be based on respect for their contribution.

Government and community policies should facilitate and encourage landless farm workers and rural workers to get some land for cultivation or expanded kitchen gardens.

Farming should be on the basis of small (and medium) farmers. Farmland ownership by corporate interests and land holdings by big landlords should not be allowed. Ceiling laws should be implemented. Land above ceiling limit should be distributed among the landless.

Diversion of food crops for production of liquor, wine, luxury foods and non-essential raw materials should be discouraged. The number one priority use of farmland should always be for ending hunger and malnutrition. Consumption of liquor, tobacco, meat, highly processed and rich luxury food should be discouraged.

In villages government can directly buy a significant part of the crop by paying immediate or even advance fair price to farmers. This part of the crop (cereals, millets, oilseeds, pulses) can be stored within the village for ration shop, Anganwadi and mid-day meal cooking. When mid-day meal is cooked for school children, it can provide at least one nutritious cooked meal daily to needy persons.

Such a food and farming system will contribute greatly to ensuring sustainable, satisfactory and creative livelihoods in farming while ensuring the availability of adequate and safe food for all. At the same time, it will also promote socio-economic equality, bio-diversity, and protection of environment and welfare of all forms of life.

12.2 Resolving Farmers' Crisis, Rural Distress

Wider aspects of the farming crisis need to be resolved and durable solutions found. There are also acute problems faced by the landless who constitute the poorest in the rural society. In this wider context, an alternative plan is proposed here for resolving the crisis of farmers and significantly reducing poverty.

We should accept an agro-ecology approach based on protection of environment, self-reliant farming and scientific utilization of local resources. This should be adopted to increase and maintain farm production at a good level. This involves careful observation of nature and natural processes. We should never disrupt them; instead we must learn from nature to improve farming and food system. Giving more attention to soil and moisture conservation and greenery is another must. This approach can drastically reduce cash costs of the farmer while opportunities of creative work are more. The work of women farmers deserves more recognition. This is particularly so in the collection, protection and use of seeds of indigenous varieties of crops and in selection of most appropriate mixed farming systems and crop rotations. Crops, trees and animal husbandry should be well integrated. Staple food crops should get first priority.

We should adopt small and cottage-scale processing of food and other crops in a big way. This will help process paddy, pulses, oilseeds, milk, spices and cotton at village and panchayat level, paving the way for several labour and skill-intensive livelihoods. In addition, crafts can be revived and strengthened. Several basic needs can be met where possible by non-polluting cottage and small industries in villages. Improved access to information technology can add to diverse livelihoods.

The food security system should be decentralized. At the local level the government purchases a share of the staple food crops at a fair price. The same should be made available to local nutrition programmes. Apart from cereals, purchase of certain amounts of vegetables, pulses, fruits, edible oils, milk and spices will be included.

Last but not the least, social reform committees should be constituted in all villages under the leadership of women and youth to work for reducing consumption of liquor and all substance abuse. There should be campaigns against untouchability, discrimination, communalism, factionalism, dowry system, needless ceremonial expenses, corruption and other social evils. These committees will also work for educational and health reform as well as transparency and governance reform.

12.3 India Needs Green Stimulus

In the wake of the Covid-19 pandemic, the crisis in the Indian economy has deepened. It has adversely affected some of the poorest sections. While the need for government policy to deliver an adequate stimulus package is felt widely, there is a wide difference of opinion regarding the precise form this should take. Half-hearted efforts such as those based on temporarily increasing the purchasing power of government employees for consumer goods cannot go far. The economy needs a much more ambitious response.

Firstly, the stimulus should be such as to provide immediate livelihood and income support to the weaker sections. It should be labour intensive and not capital intensive. Secondly, the works taken up under the stimulus should prioritize environment protection. Thirdly, this effort on a massive scale should not be a standalone effort. One should take forward this initiative in such a way that this merges with and contributes to improving future overall development.

These essential aspects should be respected in both rural and urban components of a great green stimulus.

In rural areas careful plans should be prepared involving villagers, community leaders, panchayats, local officials and activists. These should cover water conservation and harvesting, rejuvenation of vanishing or endangered small streams, rivulets, ponds and other water sources, small-scale irrigation, drainage, regeneration of degraded land including pasture and forest land, protection of forests, tree planting, protection from natural disasters, collection of traditional seeds, spread of agro-ecology approach and small-scale agro-processing.

This should be on a scale to provide significant livelihood support to about 50 million persons. At the same time, a strong base must be created for many sustainable livelihoods. Most of the immediate livelihood support should be for landless or near landless. But the entire village community will benefit from the overall improvement of environmental conditions.

A special focus should be on improving and greening degraded land. One can make available a big stretch of degraded forest land to around a hundred landless or near landless villagers. They get livelihood support for creating conducive conditions for regeneration of natural forest. Additional local species of trees can be planted. Immediate livelihood and income support is generated in these activities. At the same time, villagers get grass initially and later they can get a lot of minor forest produce from the new forest. They can get rights over the forest regenerated by them. They can keep dairy animals and cultivate small patches in and around the forest. The initial employment provided by the stimulus leads to more permanent, sustainable, land ownership-based livelihood.

Similarly, degraded land suitable for agriculture and/ or horticulture can be regenerated. Funding for all these works is available under various government programmes. The actual achievement is poor because, beyond paying salaries and meeting administrative costs, funding support for actual work is poor. There is lack of linkages in various works and departments. Comprehensive and long-term planning is often missing. There is very less involvement of local talent in planning and implementation. There is widespread corruption.

A great green stimulus should seek to overcome all these problems while increasing funding for all these works and activities. Utilization of the funds should be improved.

Regarding the urban component, the stimulus should contribute to greatly enhancing and improving, with greater participation of people in planning and implementation, works relating to water conservation and harvesting, protection of traditional water bodies, increase greenery, better drainage, steps to prevent sudden flooding, overall protection from disasters, more tree planting, digging/ maintenance of compost pits, protection of diversity and better care of parks and green areas.

Here also additional employment for millions (perhaps about 25 million people) from weakest sections should be created by the stimulus. Creative efforts should be made to link the employment to longer-term livelihood opportunities.

Such a stimulus should have an adequately long span to be able to make an effective contribution. As its formal time span nears completion, the various efforts should be integrated with regular activities and budgets so that no good initiative is disrupted or abandoned midway.

Such a stimulus will boost the overall economy. This will help significantly to reduce inequalities. It will also help improve environment protection.

Great Scientists, Skilled Farmers

In fact, in every rice growing locality, the growers themselves tell us which of their own varieties are high yielding to which they stick. But under the extension services, the definition of high yielding rice variety is different which necessarily involves a dwarfing gene and, therefore, growers' own high yielding varieties are not recognized which are estimated to be 8 or 9 percent in MP

—Dr RH Richharia
Former Director,
Central Rice Research Institute

13.1 Mangal Turbine: Neglected Innovation

If an innovation can save billions of rupees worth of diesel for farmers while also cutting down on greenhouse gas emissions, it should get top priority attention of the government. If its utility has already been confirmed time and again by the governments' own officials and experts, the case for such rapid spread becomes even stronger.

So it is a great mystery why Mangal Turbine and its innovator, farmer-scientist Mangal Singh, have been neglected by the government.

Mangal Singh grew up in a farmer family of Bundelkhand (Uttar Pradesh). As a teenager, he saw farmers of his village Bhailoni Lodh (Lalitpur district) feel disheartened when they could not arrange diesel to lift water from streams to irrigate their fields.

An idea was imprinted in the young mind to innovate a device which could lift water from streams (or small rivers, canals, nullahs) without diesel (or electricity). After a lot of experimentation, he succeeded.

The invention was named Mangal Turbine. It was first demonstrated in 1987. Mangal Singh was 40 then. It was patented as 'Mangal Water Wheel Turbine Machine' (Patent No. 177190 dated 13-11-1997) as per a Government of India gazette Notification.

This technology is described by Mangal Singh thus: The water wheel turbine machine consists of a water wheel which is firmly mounted on a steel shaft and supports on two bearing blocks fixed on foundation supports. The shaft is coupled with a suitable gearbox through universal couplings for stepping up speed of rotation. Output shaft of the gear box is coupled on one end with a centrifugal pump for lifting water and the other end is mounted with a suitable pulley for deriving power for operating any machine.... The machine can also be used for several rural works such as operating atta chakki, sugarcane, crushing, threshing and winnowing, oil expelling, chaff cutting, etc.

The Ministry of Rural Development appointed the Maithani Committee to look into various aspects of the Mangal Turbine. This committee commented: There are several variants of the Mangal Turbine but the standard device contains a water wheel of 2 meter diameter with 12 blades radially fixed to the rim. The shaft is coupled with a suitable gear box for stepping up rotation to 1,500-1,800 rpm. The output shaft of the gear box is coupled on one end with a centrifugal pump for lifting water and the other end is mounted with a suitable pulley to operate any other machine like crusher, grinder etc. By using the energy of flowing water in a stream, Mangal Turbine enables lifting of water for irrigation/drinking purposes and also produces mechanical power that can be used for various other purposes.... It is undoubtedly unparalleled in its simplicity and utility. Its cost benefit cannot be restricted to the extent of area irrigated and increase in production and income on account of that. Its benefits are multiple and multidimensional.

BK Saha, former Chief Secretary, Madhya Pradesh, wrote about it, 'I made a detailed analysis of the economic viability of the 'Wheel' and its comparative advantage vis-a-vis alternative methods of pumping water from streams and small rivers for irrigation. The system is extremely cost effective even after taking into consideration the cost of the Stop Dam. Where the Stop Dam is already available, the system is even more cost effective.'

A report of IIT-Delhi and Vigyan Shikhsha Kendra said, 'Most significant aspect is that the entire system designed by Mangal Singh is easily fabricated in the village itself, using available material and local workmanship. Besides, it requires minimal maintenance compared to other types. Expertise for maintenance is available in the village itself.... Thus, Mangal Turbine would prove a boon for fulfilling the energy need of irrigation, agro processing etc. in the rural sector wherever low water head exists in the rivers/Nallah...'

It has been estimated that if one unit of Mangal Turbine runs for 11 hours in a day, it saves 44 litres of diesel (on the basis of use of 4 litre diesel per hour by 25 HP diesel pump). Again, assuming irrigation by Mangal Turbine is done on 190 days in a year, a single unit of MT can save 8,360 litres (44x190). Over a lifetime of 15 years, one unit of MT can potentially save 125,400 litres (8,360x15). In terms of greenhouse gas emissions, this works out to 335 tonnes. This estimate by Dr Jai Shankar Singh is made on the basis of the assumption that one unit of MT will lift water from a stream which is equivalent to 25 HP diesel pump set and irrigate a command area of 50 ha. Reduction in diesel consumption and related GHG emissions can increase significantly to the extent that the Mangal Turbine is also used for processing of farm produce and other work.

Dr Sarla Gopalan, Advisor, Planning Commission, who visited the Mangal Turbine installation site near Mangal Singh's village, recommended, 'This is an excellent example of energy conservation and needs to be popularized in various other locations where advantage of flowing water is available.'

So far, this account reads like a great success story, a classic case of flowering of the technical genius of a farmer youth who focused on a leading problem around him and solved it on the basis of local resources.

Then why did things go wrong? Mangal Singh was subjected to victimization and humiliation instead of encouragement which he richly deserved. A brief answer is provided by the government's Maithani Committee Report (2011-12), 'Mangal Singh was harassed and harmed in the process of implementation of the project. This has happened not only in connection with the project under reference which was the last sanctioned by CAPART (an organization of the Government to promote rural technology). It has happened in respect of all projects sanctioned by CAPART to Mangal Singh earlier too.'

The report added, 'There is no case against Mangal Singh who needs to be compensated for the losses suffered due to advisory role played by CAPART in all the projects sanctioned to him simply because he did not "please" them! Or because he was from humble background and rural area or because he was an anti-corruption activist.'

Subsequently, Mangal Singh won court cases to get modest monetary compensation for damage caused to him. He says this is hardly adequate for all the suffering caused over two decades. Above all, his creative work was hindered again and again.

Mangal Singh, now 74, has suffered a lot. No more time should be lost in making the best possible use of his special talents. He should get adequate facilities to install Mangal Turbine in suitable places and to train young rural technicians.

The road map for the rapid spread of Mangal Turbine has been laid down by the Maithani Committee. This calls for re-installing them at places where these have been damaged after installation and to rapidly take up their spread in other places under government programmes.

The Maithani Committee's recommendations have been neglected during the last eight years by the very government which set up the panel.

The Committee said: There are some half a dozen sites where Mangal Turbines were once operating which were visited by many dignitaries and experts. But these assets have been damaged allegedly by some vested interests with the help of anti-social elements who did not like the innovation and particularly the low cost construction of check dams as the comparison was exposing their misdeeds. All these sites need to be restored with functioning Mangal Turbines. It will be of great help to the farmers of the area who are spending huge sums in operating a large number of diesel engines for irrigation.

...Mangal Turbine should be embraced by not only CAPART but all other agencies of the Government ... CAPART needs to shed all reservations about Mangal Turbine... The Ministry of Rural Development should also adopt it as a scheme to be implemented under Livelihood Mission.

It was in 1987 that the potential of Mangal Turbine was first demonstrated by Mangal Singh. Within a short time this attracted a lot of attention. Many scientists and senior officials visited the site confirming its usefulness in lifting water from streams without using either diesel or electricity.

As a development journalist I have written on this subject for years to emphasize the need for justice and adequate recognition to Mangal Singh. I visited the area to see it in operation, spoke to beneficiary farmers who praised the innovation, read the opinions of senior officials and scientists and spoke to some of them as well as studied reports and documents on the subject.

The conclusion I could draw on the basis of this effort was that we have adequate expert opinion to confirm that this device can make a major contribution in agriculture and more. This can greatly help farmers and promote rural self-reliance. But this tremendous potential has not been utilized. If it had been, great benefits would have accrued to our farmers and other villagers as well as to our country. In addition, unfortunately, tremendous injustice was done to Mangal Singh.

13.2 Big Contribution of Small Farmers

It was a pleasure to visit the garden and farm cultivated by Prabhavati and her husband Suryabhan in Dudhai village. They own only 1.5 acres of land but use it very intensively (while practising organic farming). They wisely grow a wide diversity of crops. When I started noting down the names of various crops and trees grown by them, Prabhavati laughed and remarked, 'Your notebook will fill up and yet you will not be able to write all that we grow.'

This gentle confidence is well-deserved. This couple indeed has succeeded in growing a lot of diversity in their small piece of land. From what I could see, there was paddy, *bajra* (cereals), *maruwa* (millet), groundnut, *til* (oilseeds), *lobhiya* (cowpea), *tori* (ridged gourd) or nenuwa, lemon, bottle gourd or *lauki*, *kathal* (jackfruit), guava, papaya, mango, *chakotra*, blackberries, mulberry, *mahua* (oil-nut), trees and shrubs with pest repellent properties like *neem*, *madaar* (sodom apple), *kaner* (Cascabela thevetia), trees of timber value particularly *saagwaan* (teak), several medicinal herbs, spices like ginger, *haldi* (turmeric) and even *laung* (clove) and also bamboo. Satyendra Tripathi, a co-ordinator of GEAG, said Prabhavati grows 52 crops in a year.

Prabhavati said her family, her farming and village have benefited hugely from the interaction with GEAG since the organisation came to her area about 15 years back. Earlier too she used dung as manure but this was done arbitrarily so that a lot of its nutritive value for farmland was lost. 'GEAG taught how dung should be put in a trench and composted, how green manuring can be done in a better way, how cow urine is useful and how we can do vermicomposting, how NADEP can be prepared. If we could not afford wood and cement for NADEP, we used home-grown bamboo and tree branches. Similarly, we learnt to use produce from various local trees and shrubs to prepare pest repellents.' She also has a vernicomposting unit, one of the earliest in this region.

When we visited their farm, Prabhadevi and her husband Suryabhan were busy packing the just-harvested guavas for a nearby market. We reached in good time to get a taste of the freshly plucked guavas! I couldn't help observing how gender equality had been established in this family and, to some extent, gender roles had even reversed without causing any tensions. Prabhavati played a leading role in answering our questions and taking us around the garden. She was better dressed and more articulate. Suryabhan did not resent this.

Prabhavati is now a member of the core group of GEAG. She is also a master trainer and has travelled far and wide including Delhi, Lucknow and Wardha. Her small farm has been visited by senior officials.

Moving to the main settlement of the village, we met several women farmers who confirmed the many sided benefits that have accrued to them due to GEAG. Shanti Devi is the Secretory of a self-help group. The loan she took enabled her to improve vegetable cultivation in her fields and to own a shop where she sells her produce. She grows cauliflower, cabbage, onion, peas, tomatoes, potato, *lobhiya* (cowpea), *nenuwa* (ridged gourd), bottle gourd, pumpkin, *haldi*... the list goes on.

Kusumawati is the Treasurer of the local federation and runs the Kisan Vidyalaya in her village. As though this was not enough, she has also been selected as an ASHA health worker. Her husband is a Home Guard in Gorakhpur. Household duties and the care of children besides looking after their small field falls on Kusumavati. Wearing many hats, she is extremely busy although she is still economically hard pressed.

Two interesting men I met in this village are Baijnath, a master trainer of organic farming methods, and Satya Ram, the village pradhan who offers good co-operation to various GEAG-inspired initiatives.

The extent to which the agricultural practices promoted

by GEAG can benefit small and marginal farmers is evident from the farm of Ramrati. This 50-plus woman (along with her husband Rambahal) is reputed to grow 32 crops in a year (not mentioning fruit trees). According to accounts kept by GEAG activists, during last year her expenses and earnings were in the ratio of 1:13. On a farm of just one acre owned by her family (sometimes she also leases half acre or less of land), she has been able to earn about Rs 33,600 apart from feeding a nutritious, organic diet to an 11-member family.

Before the advent of GEAG, she concentrated on rice and wheat. Now, in addition, she grows sugarcane, banana, turai, potato, cauliflower, cabbage, ramdana, rajma, bakla, latra pulse, moong, peas, methi, spinach, carrot, radish (up to 2.5 feet long), parval, kundru, karela, lobhiya, maize, cucumber, kakri, okra, mustard, garlic, ginger, guava, mango, anar, kathal, groundnuts, dhaniya, jimikand, arbi,.. She has four animals: a bullock, a buffalo and two buffalo calves. All the cultivation is done using organic manure and home-made pest repellents.

Ramrati is not just a model farmer. She has taken up multiple responsibilities. She is the Treasurer of local federation, a member of the Greater Federation, co-ordinator of a farming school and Secretary of a SHG called Ashtbhuji. She is also a master trainer for mixed farming practised by her.

Other women also spoke about how they have benefited from improved farming practices as well as SHGs. Sudhara has used a loan to start a tea and snacks shop. She also used a loan for the medical treatment of her son who had an accident. Shanti leased in some land for extra farming. Her group has purchased utensils for cooking food for weddings which are rented out.

In India, the number of farmers who have just about two acres of land is very large. If even such a small plot of land can be used in such innovative ways as to provide adequate income, then this is a matter of great hope indeed.

This optimism increases if such success is achieved on farmland which earlier was known to be low yielding or infertile. The success of Suresh Mallick and his wife Shobhavati is even more remarkable as it has been achieved on what was earlier considered to be the lowest category land on which hardly anything was likely to grow. Today, this land is smiling on almost every inch with greenery brought by highly diverse plant species.

The harbinger of this is a short, slightly built but alert and innovative farmer named Suresh who has been exposed to many adversities and injustices in life. These could have broken the spirit of any other man but not Suresh. He has emerged from them to become a symbol of hope for India's small farmers.

Earlier Suresh had an opportunity to be a Gandhian social activist working with leaders like Narayan Desai and Manmohan Chaudhary. Perhaps it was the spirit of optimism and working for a wider social cause which he imbibed and which enabled him to overcome many adversities.

Suresh could think of many brilliant applications of the technology of organic farming propagated by SVA, the organisation with which he is closely associated now in Chata village (Naupara district, Odisha). He has been helped by the considerable grafting skills he acquired in Gujarat. At the same time, he gives equal credit to his wife Shobhavati who works with him on their farm.

Suresh believes firmly in organic agriculture. This helps to reduce the farming costs. A lot of attention is given to preparing adequate compost, vermi-compost and organic sprays which help to keep away pests and diseases while also helping plants to grow. The use of plentiful, high quality composts has made the once unproductive land hugely fertile.

Suresh places emphasis on growing a wide diversity of food crops and plants including cereals, pulses, vegetables, fruits and spices. As all these have to be grown within a small plot of land, he makes the best possible use of scarce land and water. Ginger and turmeric are grown under the shadow of mango trees to protect them from heat stress and make good use of available space.

On their two acres, Suresh and Shobhavati have been able to grow paddy, pulses, mangoes, oranges, bananas, papayas, coconut, lemons, jackfruit, amla, beans, bitter gourd, carrots, sugarbeet, onions, turmeric, ginger, chilly, coriander, supari, pomegranates and other crops. Mango and lemon trees have also been planted.

Bhaja and Savitri cultivate their 4-acre farm on the outskirts of the village in such a productive way that it not only provides highly nourishing and healthy food to the five-member family but also fetches a net income of over Rs 15,000 a month (Nuapara).

Earlier Bhaja and Savitri used some agri-chemicals but

now they have shifted entirely to organic farming. As Savitri says, 'Organic food is definitely more tasty and healthy. There is more demand for organically grown produce.'

Organic farming has enabled this tribal household to reduce its costs. The family makes compost and pest repellent liquid on their farm using largely the resources available free on their farm or in the village.

Another reason their net income has gone up is the diversity of crops and animals on their small farm. The family grows paddy, moong (pulse), onion, tomatoes, sugarcane, pumpkin, maize, coriander, blackberries, lemons, mangoes, tamarind, papaya, bamboo, subabool (for fodder), radish, beans, belfruit, amla, bananas, mustard, turmeric, local green leafy vegetables and several other produce. This farm gets dry fruit from chiraunji, oil from karanj oilseed (also from mahuwa seeds), medicine from bahera and other plants and toothbrush from babool trees. They have three cows and two bullocks and calves each.

13.3 Traditional Seeds also Give High Yields

The most important feature of the 'green revolution' phase of Indian agriculture was the introduction of HYV seeds. There can be several types of High Yield Variety (HYV) seeds. For example, in Madhya Pradesh and Chhattisgarh, some indigenous rice varieties have been found to give very high yields even by traditional methods of cultivation. However, in the official programmes of improved agriculture in India, generally only those (dwarf, non-lodging) varieties which gave high yields when fed by chemical fertilisers were included. Therefore, we should call them HRVs (High Response Varieties) rather than HYVs. For the sake of comparability with other publications, we also use the expression 'HYV's.

During early 1970, at an early stage of the green revolution in Madhya Pradesh (which then included Chhattisgarh), eminent scientist Dr Richharia's research revealed that several indigenous rice varieties gave high yields without the use of chemical fertilizers. This information is provided in Table 5.

Table 5 Potential of some high yielding varieties of Indian rice varieties with special reference to Madhya Pradesh and Chhattisgarh

S. No.	Original Rice Variety	Improved version no.	Paddy kg/Ha.	Rice Grade	Maturity
1.	Lalloo	Bd.12	7024	Medium Fine	Early
2.	Dhour	Bd. 23	6136	Medium Fine	Early
3.	Koyalari	Bd. 811	7350	Coarse	Early
4.	Nungi	Bd. 813	7623	Coarse	Early
5.	Cross 116	Bd. 30	4000	Coarse	Medium
6.	Kalam	Bd. 368	5510	Medium Fine	Medium
7.	Beni Kath	Bd. 452	4080	Short fine	Medium
8.	Tedhi Banko	Bd. 207	6290	Long fine	Late
9.	Kala Mali	Bd. 108	7600	Coarse	Late
10.	Safri	Bd. 200	5520	Medium	Late
11.	Dubraj	Bd. 153	4958	Medium fine	Late
12.	Tedhi Banko	Bd. 207	6250	Long fine	Late
13.	Kariya Chini	Bd. 366	5550	Medium fine	Late

Dr Richharia emphasised that wisdom of local farmers regarding diverse rice varieties should be utilised as the major resource for improving rice cultivation. He emphasised that rice farmers who possess intimate knowledge of their rice varieties should be involved in the research effort, 'even to guide us with their inherent gift'.

'A special advantage associated with indigenous high yielding rice germplasm identified for different tracts and situations is that it possesses a good level of resistance to environmental stress and common diseases and pests, coupled with local preference for palatability.'

While healthy indigenous varieties were denied recognition as HYVs, excessively disease and pest prone varieties were readily recognised as HYVs and propagated very rapidly.

The massive damage became so worrying that a special task force on rice breeding was constituted of eminent experts in 1979 to examine this issue. These experts met at the CRRI in February. Dr Richharia was called back from his retirement to head this Task Force as his advice was considered invaluable. Its report stated, 'Most of the HYVs are derivatives of T(N) 1 or I.R. 8 and, therefore, have the dwarfing gene of dee-geo-woo-gen. This narrow genetic base has created alarming uniformity, causing vulnerability to diseases and pests. Most of the released varieties are not suitable for typical uplands and low lands which together constitute about 75 percent of the total rice area of the country.'

Clearly great damage has been caused. There has been a heavy bias against traditional seeds in agriculture research and extension efforts of the government as well as corporates. This needs to be corrected.

13.4 Dr Richharia's Role in Indian Agriculture

In debates on agriculture in India, Dr RH Richharia's name inevitably comes up though establishment persons and powerful interests would prefer to avoid this. Dr Richharia was extremely learned and distinguished, certainly the top rice scientist from India. Many believe he should have occupied the topmost position in farm research at a critical time of India's agricultural history. But he was unjustly deprived of this because he was firm in defending and protecting the interests of farmers and his country. If he had succeeded, this would have benefitted not only India but the agriculture of other developing countries as well.

When the critical decision to arbitrarily bring in the green revolution seeds was being taken, Dr Richharia stood up bravely to oppose this. He insisted on an alternative strategy based in improved indigenous varieties. It was a strategy capable of giving good yields without any dependence on chemical fertilizers and pesticides. Instead of being rewarded for his views, Dr Richharia was unceremoniously deprived of his official senior position and victimized. Those responsible for his victimization were glorified as the saviors of Indian agriculture.

At a later stage, when Dr Richharia again got a senior official position, he opposed the efforts of multinational companies to gain control of indigenous varieties of rice. Once again he was victimized and removed from his post.

Radheylal Herlal Richharia had a very promising start

to his distinguished career as a farm scientist. He completed his doctorate at Cambridge in less than two years though he had gone on a shoestring budget and worked and stayed there in very difficult conditions. Before leaving Cambridge, he went to say goodbye to his professor who said, 'So many scholars who return from Cambridge to India hold many prestigious posts and publish many learned papers. But I do not know how many of them actually strive to help the farmers of India. The real test is whether your work will be of real help to the poor farmers of your country.'

Richaria was born in 1909 in Nandanvara village of Seoni Malwa Tehsil in Hoshangabad district of (what is now) Madhya Pradesh. His father, Herlal Richharia, was the headmaster of a school and also the postmaster. Always keen to do some new work, he experimented with growing several vegetables in his garden.

He had careful and painstaking methods of growing vegetables. In some cases, he would not use any direct irrigation, preferring instead to use the percolation method, saying that this way the land would make more efficient use of water. Then, in the case of some vegetables which grow as creepers, he would insist that they get the support of a neem tree. The belief was that the vegetables would absorb some of the medicinal properties of the neem. His curious son looked on eagerly at his father's work, fascinated by all the interesting information. He learnt to admire and respect the wealth of wisdom available in the villages.

He was equally fascinated by the *adivasis* with whom his father had great rapport. He was fascinated by 'Rani Sahiba', who seemed a tribal headwoman. The tribals collected chiraunji seeds and not only brought this to his father but also prepared beautiful ways of storing them unspoilt. The tribal visitors revealed their rich wisdom of trees and plants.

Before he left his village for higher education, Richaria had imbibed enough knowledge about the wisdom of farmers in general and tribals in particular. It enabled him to retain his humility and attitude of respect for them even when he earned his doctorate from Cambridge.

Richaria pursued further education at Balaghat, Varanasi and Nagpur. From Nagpur he went to Cambridge. His first job was also at Nagpur – as oil seeds specialist for Central Province (1931-42). He moved to the Agricultural Research Institute and Agriculture College at Sabour (Bhagalpur, Bihar) where he held various positions and developed his keen interest for rice which was to become a lifelong passion. He showed his flair for field level work by motivating students to do work in fields and dairies, thereby earning themselves a rich breakfast of *halwa* and milk!

He started pioneering work on preparing quality fibre from the waste straw of linseed plant, a work which drew the attention of several eminent persons. He remained in Bihar for 17 long years (1942 to 1959).

In 1959, he became Director of the Central Rice Research Institute (CRRI) at Cuttack, Orissa. A rival who desired the post manipulated a strike by employees. This hurdle was soon overcome. Dr Richharia was able to establish the CRRI as one of the foremost centres of rich research in the world.

However, vested interests conspired against him to disrupt

his work. He left the CRRI in 1967. Despite his seniority, he was unjustly deprived of the opportunity to become the Director General of the Indian Council of Agricultural Research (ICAR). The main reason for his unceremonious ouster was that he had opposed the arbitrary introduction of green revolution seeds and insisted on rice development based on improved indigenous varieties. He was on the verge of achieving a big breakthrough based on this. All his preparations and wisdom were dismantled to welcome the green revolution varieties which, Dr Richharia warned even at an early stage, were prone to diseases and pests.

In 1971, he was recalled from retirement to head the Madhya Pradesh Rice Research Institute at Raipur and also to function as Agriculture Adviser to the Government of Madhya Pradesh. Here, during 1971-76, he did pioneering work of great value with special reference to preserving and protecting the agricultural heritage of tribal farmers. Again, vested interests manipulated things to deprive him of opportunities when his work had reached a critical stage. The powerful interests wanted multinational companies to gain control of the collection of indigenous varieties made with great care by Dr. Richharia and his colleagues with the help of farmers.

From 1978 to 1996, Dr Richharia, now deprived of all facilities for scientific work, continued his work against all odds at his residence and at a farm located a few miles from his residence in Bhopal.

In 1971, Dr Richharia lost his wife, Jaiamba, who had been his greatest source of strength. Around 1982 he lost a son. In 1983, he was requested by Prime Minister

Indira Gandhi to prepare an action plan for improving rice production. This he did with great dedication. But following Gandhi's assassination, this plan was ignored. In 1984, he became a victim of the Bhopal gas tragedy. The man who had spoken all his life against the hazards of chemical pesticides himself became a victim. In December 1984 he had a heart attack, leaving him very weak.

He withstood all these tragedies and shocks to continue his work. Slowly information about his work and its importance became clear to the press, voluntary agencies and people's organisations. Reports about his accomplishments started appearing in newspapers, magazines and journals. Voluntary agencies requested him to visit their areas and tell people about his work. He was invited to important gatherings in Malaysia, Indonesia, Nepal and elsewhere.

Despite numerous adversities, he wrote a very important book on clonal propagation technology. A new edition of his old book, *Rices of India*, co-authored with S Govindswamy, was published.

Dr Richharia died in 1996 at age 87. In his last days, he was working on an encyclopaedia of rice germplasm of Madhya Pradesh in which 19,000 cultivars of rice were being listed. This is the result of several years of collection and identification of rice cultivars. He was also completing the botanical survey work with special reference to rice and rice research conducted by him during the 70s in MPRRI. He continued his tireless work in preparing a Botanical Dictionary of useful plants in India. This work began in 1946-47 and over 8,000 entries had been made (with available chromosome family name, botanical name, popular English and Hindi names, uses and other information). In addition, he continued to carry out botanical research on his farm and worked on evolving interesting concepts such as those of rice garden and rural gene banks.

All this work he did with minimum help and support from outside. Some help was extended by agricultural universities in Madhya Pradesh and voluntary agencies/ institutions by agreeing to publish a part of his voluminous work.

In the course of his careful, painstaking and brilliant research extending over six decades, Dr Richharia's work was distinguished by some important features:

1. Respect for wisdom and knowledge of ordinary farmers, especially tribals.
2. Deep concern for small and poor farmers, an understanding of their resource constraints and efforts to make available low cost, local resource based technology involving no chemical pesticides.
3. Respect for indigenous genetic base of rice and concern to preserve the indigenous varieties. Efforts to increase rice productivity should be based mainly on indigenous varieties. Towards this end, he made a great discovery of the hidden potential of indigenous varieties, their high productivity and superb food qualities. In Madhya Pradesh and Chhattisgarh he collected (or guided the collection of) over 17,000 cultivars of rice.
4. Firm determination to protect the interests of ordinary farmers and his country from forces of imperialism and readiness to accept any sacrifice for this higher cause.

His outstanding professional work, honesty and sacrifice are immensely inspiring. All of this is much needed today as the onslaught of multinational companies and imperialism has become worse than before. India and other developing countries need more and more scientists like Dr Richharia. At the same time, we must try we need to improve the overall systems so that such scientists do not have to suffer time and again. The importance of this work which protects the organic content of soil while minimizing the use of external inputs which destroy soil has increased in times of climate change.

13.5 A Neglected Plan of Great Potential

Rice is by far the most important crop and the most important food of India. At a time when there are increasing concerns about food security, it is of the greatest importance to increase rice yields significantly while keeping down the costs of cultivation.

'*A Silent Rice Revolution - A Specific Plan of Action for Increase in Productivity of Rice*' formulated by Dr Richharia appears as a ray of hope. This was formulated by Dr Richharia at the request of the Prime Minister's Office in 1983-84. However, after the assassination of Indira Gandhi in 1984, the plan got neglected. When this writer met him well before his death in 1996, he still had hopes that one day this document will prove helpful for rice farmers and farming. In any case, this will remain an invaluable document for all concerned. Climate change related threats have made this document even more relevant and important.

First, Dr Richharia identified the factors which have retarded the increase in rice productivity despite so much increase in investments in the form of fertilisers, pesticides, irrigation, research and extension. He outlines his plan in brief with four basic components -

(1) Rice development to be based on the rich diversity of indigenous varieties which should be saved on farmers' fields. A lot of priority and attention should be given to this aspect.
(2) A highly decentralised extension approach.
(3) Large-scale adoption of clonal propagation technique to spread improved indigenous varieties.
(4) Very high levels of involvement of rice farmers with special emphasis on encouraging those who have special skills and interest in protection and promotion of diverse indigenous varieties.

Said Dr Richharia: The main constraint has been the hurried introduction of the undesirable new rice material, the HYVs (dwarfs) on which we based our strategy, forgetting at the same time unexpected drought situations, under which the HYVs lowered the yields. In addition, under heavy fertilization and irrigation, the HYVs proved to be susceptible to diseases and pests which cannot be controlled easily, thus again pointing towards reduction of yield. Further, unlike wheat and sugarcane, the concept of 'wider adaptability' in rice has a limited scope for application (not exceeding 10 percent of the rice area). This has naturally led to local preferences of different types of rice and socio-economic adjustments, developed in course of time.

According to Dr Richharia, when the base is itself weak (meaning new rice material) a mansion built on it must collapse.

At another place, he wrote: The most immediate and major cause can be attributed to frequent replacements of the adapted rice varieties in a locality, partly or fully. This is because the agro-ecological balance has been disturbed in the environment in respect of the existing germplasm which had been built up in the course of time for centuries by the natural process of empirical breeding and selection establishing ecological balance in different environments, what in modern times can be interpreted as 'ecological breeding'.

Fortunately, indigenous high yielding varieties adapted to local environment are available in the country. In a survey carried out in Madhya Pradesh between 1971-74, 8 percent of the indigenous rice types were observed to fall under the category of high yielding types, fixing the minimum limit of 3,705 kg/Ha.

In view of this, there is a need to redefine 'HYVs' which hitherto have been officially identified only with the exotic dwarf fertiliser - responsive varieties.

At a national symposium on increasing rice yields in Kharif (Monsoon season) held at Cuttack, the rice workers agreed that the time is ripe to redefine the term High Yielding Variety (HYV) as a high yielding variety for a particular environment possessing suitable plant-type characters for that condition which may not be suitable for other environments. 'A (rice) variety irrespective of its plant and/stature giving significantly higher yield over the local or regional average yield under farmer's condition may be defined as a high yielding variety (HYV).'

To emphasise the point further, the Directorate of Rice Development had issued a paper, '*Need for a National Policy on Rice*' (1972). It said: The new varieties of rice should be as good as the (current varieties) older ones in local adaptability and some characteristics but not inferior in any character. It is our experience that when we try to recommend a variety which is a compromise between a high yield and some other character in which the local (older) varieties are superior that we run into trouble. We should not over-emphasise yield but should insist upon a minimum aroma and cooking quality as rice is the only cereal which is directly consumed without much change in the form of its grain.

Dr Richharia recommended: It is high time that the country's 1964-65 breeding programme which nearly stands suspended to exploit the rice indigenous rice germplasm is also resumed in light of the observations recorded above, when about 445 improved varieties, bred for specific stress situations, showing environmental resistance to diseases and pests were available, and would be still available, in the country. It is not too late and the strategy formulated in this programme, mainly based on our rice genetic resources may be accepted which also contemplates that the indigenous germplasm in its hybridized form (hybrid rices) has also a bright future to enhance rice productivity.

Selection work (genetic upgrading) with indigenous rice types was resumed by Dr Richharia in 1968 after leaving Cuttack. About 1,500 improved types (improved versions) and eleven composites were developed and made available by 1978 selected from about 7,800 principal indigenous rice cultivars. The approach was to release this hidden production force which remains unnoticed, unrecognised and confined to certain localities with individual growers.

For high yield potential genetic upgrading of their adapted rice varieties (indigenous rice germplasm), with certain manipulation, such as the evolution of new hybrids and exploiting hybrid vigorously utilizing pure material of local types, is the only course left for speedy recovery of loss, to stabilise rice production at a higher level, instead of waiting to replace our rice by other rice material of doubtful nature which may or may not get adapted to stabilise yields in the environments under which rice grows in variable situations in India.

In the area of research as well as extension, Dr Richharia recommends a highly decentralised approach. This, he emphasises, is inherent in the nature of the rice plant. 'If we were to think of a single characteristic feature of the rice plant which yields food for millions, it cannot be anything else but its variability in the form of thousands of its cultivars, spread in India and in other rice growing belts of the world. This is because of the rice plants' flexible genetic make-up and mutational power of adaptation.'

So he recommends the establishment of a wide network of 'adaptive rice centres' in all rice-growing areas.

'The adaptive rice centres will be the custodians of all local rice cultivars in respective localities, assembled immediately, supplemented if necessary, by the already available materials of the locality at different research centres. They will be maintained under their natural habitat to safeguard the future. They will be known as local treasuries of rice germplasm (a term suggested by Dr Frankel of Australia).'

The functions of the centres will be:

(a) To maintain the evolved rice genetic material for future studies and use as it is practically impossible to retain it in its original form at a central place in India or abroad. It can only be maintained in its original condition at its natural habitat seeking help of the rice growers themselves.

(b) To educate the young farmers to appreciate the value and importance of their own material adding new ones as their hobby.

On the basis of his wide experience, Dr Richharia says: I, invariably found in rice areas several rice growers taking keen interest in their local rice varieties as they are very much absorbed in them and they have all praise for them, so much so that they trace back the history of individual rice varieties to their ancestry. With their utility such selected and devoted rice farmers will be put in charge of the centres. I also observed that some of them identify their rice varieties in their own way (not in terms of the modern knowledge of Botany) which amount to thousands. This inherent and intuitional facility of selection and maintenance of thousands of rice cultivars gradually being accumulated and descended upon for unknown centuries, ever since rice first originated must be preserved and exploited for the advantage of the present generation and to ensure the safety of those still unborn.

'On the practical side a beginning may be made in MP where upgrade material already exists in the form of about 1,500 improved types made from growers' own rice cultivars which can be distributed in different centres for work to be started immediately, to obtain advantage as early as possible and to prepare the hybrid material for the next season.'

On the basis of his experience in Madhya Pradesh, Dr Richharia stresses that women will prove to be the most important link in introducing this technology. At the Adaptive Rice Research Centre in Baronda, Dr Richharia noticed that women workers absorb new methods and ideas very quickly. Here he specially promoted some women workers as supervisors for managing the germplasm of over 17,000 rice cultivars in the field and the practice of clonal propagation.

It will also be demonstrated that the healthy seeds, obtained by clonal propagation for a full crop of rice to follow, give nearly 20 percent higher production for any rice variety. Further hybrid clones for exploiting hybrid vigour can be obtained. Hybridization work will be carried out by trained field workers of the adaptive centres.

Whereas clonal propagation in rice as a means of raising pure seeds to offer 20 percent higher production and the extension of this technology to exploit hybrid vigour to obtain 50 percent increased yields remain unexploited. A great discovery of immense value is left unheeded, in the form of 19,000 rice cultivars coupled with their 1,500 improved versions representing intense variability, assembled from the least understood rice areas of MP

In a major part of the country, the rice crop is ruined by drought and flood conditions. In this context, Dr Richharia's plan is all the more invaluable as it incorporates resistance to floods as well as drought conditions, not to mention disease and pest invasions.

Dr Richharia's documents mention several drought-resistant indigenous varieties discovered in the course of field work in Chhattisgarh region and above all the immense diversity of the rice varieties. A special advantage of this in distress situations such as drought is that while some varieties suffer, some survive; so yield doesn't go below a certain level. Regarding floods, the clonal propagation method offers special advantages. It has been demonstrated that rice clones show resistance to submergence.

Dr Richharia expressed his support for organic farming and several local practices of farmers. He wrote that under this plan 'the agronomic practices such as biasi, rotation of crops, mixed cropping will remain common and will not be disturbed, emphasis being on the use of organic manures such as compost, green manure, neem cakes and oil cakes'.

Dr Richharia attached 17 documents based on his earlier research to support his plan while submitting it to the Prime Minister. In addition, he mentioned his Encyclopedia of Rice Cultivars on which he was still working. He also offered his services on an honorary basis to implement this plan.

However, the collections of improved rice varieties he mentioned (mostly arising from his own work and the work of his colleagues) may not be available to the same extent today. Similarly, the knowledge of indigenous varieties in villages may be comparatively less now. However, this is all the more reason why the implementation of this plan should not be delayed any further. The passage of time may make such a task and initiative even more difficult.

Farmers' Movement in India

Hence farmers have good reason for concluding that the three laws create a framework for moving away from a reasonably protective system to one dominated by big business interests having close links with ruling regimes, not even giving farmers the protection of normal civil courts if things go wrong with them, making the situation very uncertain and difficult in times of rising costs.

—Bharat Dogra

14.1 A Comprehensive Analysis of Three Controversial Farm Laws

It is rare for any legislation to become the rallying point of such large-scale and prolonged opposition as the three farm laws enacted in India in 2020. The farmers labeled the legislation as 'kala kanoon' (black laws) and protested in biggest ever farmers' movement.

The three laws have rather pompous, pretentious titles but essentially sought to change the existing systems of farm production (giving a push towards facilitation of contract farming) as well as storage and marketing of farm produce. Several eminent experts lent their support to the key demand of the farmers' movement for the repeal of these laws.

A comprehensive analysis of the many aspects and impacts of these farm laws is needed. To appreciate the implications of these laws, it is important to look at the background and perspective of the wider farming situation in India and the world. Without such an understanding, the full implications of these laws cannot be understood. We also need to look a little beyond the present debate on the farm laws to examine the policies we really need.

There is a deep and widespread crisis of world farming and food systems linked mainly to the quest of powerful corporates' interest to dominate. These interests, who seek super profits, are able to secure the collusion of several governments and key persons in policy and implementation. Together, they make a deadly combination.

They promote policies which relentlessly increase the sale of their expensive seeds and inputs, breaking the self-reliance of farmers and increasing their dependence and costs, regardless of adverse impacts of these inputs on the environment. At the same time, the corporate interests try relentlessly to increase their grip on crop processing, trade and marketing to get a mammoth share of the total market receipts.

The key to securing guarantee of high corporate profits is to secure dominance at various levels and to secure a legal base for this dominance. Hence, there have been endless new laws of patents, trade and farming contracts in recent years.

Their machinations create increasing problems for family farms or small and medium farmers in many countries. They are increasingly brought under pressure to increase their farm expenses while their share of market receipts is reduced greatly by corporate interests.

The ever-increasing greed for more profits and higher market share on the part of big corporate interests plays havoc with the objective of providing safe and healthy food to all.

Incredibly, all this takes place on a vast scale in the name of development and progress. To make the system based on manipulation work, the system tries to co-opt some of the bigger and influential farmers. The governments keep announcing some temporary concession or relief for farmers, all the more so at election times. The big corporates' increasing dominance of food and farming systems marginalizes the bulk of small farmers, harming environment, health and sustainability. From time to time, exploited farmers unite to demand justice. Unable to challenge the bigger forces, their demands have rather narrow aims.

In addition, there is the impact of multilateral and bilateral trade treaties by which food and farming systems are impacted. Here too the richest countries, in flagrant violation of the principle of correcting historic injustice, as big agribusiness companies use these to inflict further injustice and constraints on farmers of developing countries.

All this has been experienced in the context of farmers of India as well, the overwhelming majority of whom are small and medium farmers. They have been reeling under the combined impact of zooming costs, marketing problems and escalating debts. Compulsions of electoral democracy prompted many governments to create some protective structure for them. This too is under the threat of trade agreements (notably WTO) and big corporate interests want a wider and unrestricted role for their expansion. They would like to have a legal guarantee for this before making bigger investments.

It is in this wider context that the debate on the farm laws should be seen. The current regime in India is known to be willing to push corporate interests, particularly of some crony capitalists considered close to the powers that be.

One of these three laws relates to facilitating a much bigger role for contract farming. The worldwide experience of small farmers and family farms regarding contract farming for big business concerns has been that of increasing tensions, increasing costs and feeling cheated time and again. The law to promote contract farming has attracted specific criticism also for terms biased in favour of corporate interests and for leaving dispute resolution outside the normal civil court jurisdiction.

The other two laws seek to create a new framework of untaxed, unrestricted purchases by private business outside the area of officially designated market areas for farm produce (APMCs or Agriculture Produce Marketing

Committees) while removing existing restrictions on excess stocking and hoarding of even essential, staple foods by private traders and companies. These have been rightly criticized by farmers as a strong signal of moving away from government protected and regulated MSP based system.

On the other hand, the government has said that it has no intention of dismantling the APMC-MSP based existing system (which plays a limited effective role in the entire country but a more dominating role in the green revolution states like Punjab and Haryana). Yes, the government may not officially announce dismantling of this system, but the farmers say rightly that its recent laws send strong signals of gradually moving away from this by providing unrestricted, untaxed new marketing avenues to big business.

Hence, farmers have good reason for concluding that the three laws create a framework for moving away from a reasonably protective system to one dominated by big business interests having close links with the ruling regime, not even giving farmers the protection of normal civil courts if things go wrong. This makes the situation very uncertain and difficult in times of rising costs.

In conditions of widespread poverty and low purchasing power of a large number of households, there is no guarantee that the market by itself would give high priority to producing adequate staple food needed for keeping away hunger and malnutrition. So this has to be ensured by a protective system based on MSP-government procurement-PDS (public distribution system) and nutrition schemes. But when the government moves away from protective farm and food system to one dominated by big agribusiness interests of national and global food/ farming system, with a huge capacity to hoard and speculate, then both production and marketing will move away from reducing hunger to maximizing profits.

The new trends unleashed by these laws move towards profiteering and speculation, that too in increasingly globalized systems. As more production takes place in conditions governed by contract system and dominated by big companies with global reach, production will be pushed by global profits and speculation and not by the needs of hungry and malnourished people in the country.

The present condition of Indian agriculture, particularly in so-called leading green revolution areas, is not at all good from the point of view of sustainability and environment protection. The situation certainly needs to be improved. But the trends unleashed by the new laws are likely to lead to further deterioration rather than any improvement.

Cropping patterns and methods of production need to be in keeping with the needs of soil health and water conservation as well as other aspects of protection of environment and bio-diversity. Contract farming dictated by big companies pays scant regards to all this. It often imposed highly resource-extractive cropping patterns and technologies. Their profits ignore social and environmental costs. Agribusiness companies operating in global contexts are notorious in looting and scooting as they plunder the resources of a region and then move to a new area, leaving behind ravaged land and depleted water aquifers.

There has been a strong feeling that under the impact

of global and national corporate interests, the Indian government intrudes rather too heavily in areas like agriculture for which decisions should instead be taken at the level of states and Panchayati Raj (rural decentralization) units. This trend increased with these three overbearing new farm laws. A more specific complaint was that state earnings from APMC/mandi taxes will decrease and development work supported by these earnings will suffer too.

These farm laws were also criticized as undemocratic as the necessary consultations with state governments, Panchayati Raj institutions, farmers' organizations and independent experts were not held. These were introduced first as ordinances, objectionable in itself. The process of referring them to the Parliamentary Committee, which would have provided one way of consultations with stakeholders, was ignored. The passing of the law in the Rajya Sabha had peculiar undemocratic features which were opposed by opposition parties and attracted several adverse comments.

As even ministers and government representatives have admitted, amendments were needed in these laws. An issue of debate was whether the farmers should accept the amendments or stick to their demand for repeal. The farmers' movement was steadfast in asking for a repeal. Supporting this stand, a letter by ten eminent economists stated, 'Amending a few clauses will not be sufficient to address the concerns rightly raised by farmers...We appeal that the government withdraw these acts.' This unanimous view of these senior economists, who have served in government-supported and other institutions and are known for their commitment to justice and public interest, is thus similar to the view of the farmers.

Beyond the debate on these laws, several issues need to be addressed. There is a strong need for agricultural progress based on justice and protection of environment, a social-ecological approach. Solutions have to be found in a much wider paradigm than one limited mainly by narrow economic concerns. Welfare and equality aspects of landless rural households should also get adequate attention.

These writers recommended early for immediate repeal of these three farm laws, lifting of all cases against farmer activists, followed in due course by much wider measures for resolving the rural crisis on the basis of justice and environment protection.

14.2 Repeal Needed, Wider Vision is Needed

Despite the initial obstinate refusal of the Union government to repeal the farm laws, there was increasing consensus among people that the legislation must go.

However, on the other question of MSP, the situation is less clear. To seek greater clarity, let us examine two different situations of farming.

In the first, farmers try their very best to reduce economic, ecological and social costs of farming by making best use of local free resources and possibilities while minimizing or avoiding use of polluting chemical fertilizers. Apart from producing healthy food, they protect soil and conserve water. The farmers are also caring about the needs and aspirations of landless farm workers.

In this situation, high priority can certainly be given to providing a government legal guarantee that a remunerative and satisfactory price will be paid for all farm produce. Even if there is surplus, the government should try its best to buy and pay this fair price as it will not be difficult to find a big export market for this healthy produce once domestic needs are met. The government should facilitate this further by making big allocations also for water and soil conservation, protection of forests and pastures, as well as providing a lot of off-season employment to landless workers, marginal farmers and women in such work. Overall conditions for this can be improved further by banning GM crops and supporting research and extension of social agro-ecology.

In the second situation, farmers indiscriminately use chemical fertilizers and pesticides, exploit water resources recklessly, exhaust soil fertility by inflicting too intensive farming, destroy organic content and micro-organisms of soil rapidly, quickly embrace hazardous technologies like GM crops, do not give much attention to protecting village greenery and are exploitative towards landless farm workers, tenants and sharecroppers. In the process, they contribute to deepening the risks of climate change.

Now it is not at all clear why the wider society or the government should encourage such farming by a regime of assured price guarantee. In fact, such farming, highly remunerative price guarantees for farm produce will be socially harmful.

In practical life such extreme situations may be less visible and a mixed situation may be more likely. But still, we can see whether an actual situation is close to the first or second model. Even in the second model, farmers are not to blame. What they are practicing is more likely to be the result of wrong policies of the government which have lured them away from traditional farming, plus the worse record of big business and their local dealers.

The more basic point here is that in the second situation the main issue is the need for moving to a more sustainable system of ecologically protective and justice-based farming. The role of the government is to facilitate this change, undoing its previous mistakes. One important way forward may be to make financial grants to all those farmers who make this change. Once this change takes place, they must get a guarantee of a remunerative price.

Food is the most basic need. Producing safe, healthy food in sustainable, protective ways is the most noble work. So spending huge parts of the government budget for this is fully justified. But asking the government to spend in a big way to support ecologically destructive, unsustainable systems which produce food whose safety and health benefits are doubtful is not justified.

However, these more complex issues are often forgotten as there is an inclination at various levels for a populist approach. So those supporting the farmers' movement often find it convenient to extend total support instead of carefully channelizing the upsurge towards a more desirable direction. They should not forget the big risk that if highly extractive systems are supported by big subsidies and budgets, these ecologically harmful methods get strengthened.

14.3 Ecologically Protective Farming

The farmers' movement in India has a historically important role in protecting the small (and medium) farmer base of agriculture. In recent times, the movement has done well to oppose the corporatization trends as these ultimately present a threat to small farmers.

However, there is one crucial aspect which should get a more central role in the demands and aspirations of the farmers. This relates to much greater emphasis on ecologically protective farming. There is growing realization all over the world that organic and natural farming can provide good yields and productivity while helping to lower economic costs significantly. In India, this aspect is very significant. The crisis of many small and medium farmers has been caused mainly by fast escalating expenses on externally purchased industrial inputs. The pattern of organic farming in the country which needs to be promoted is the one which avoids expensive certification procedures while making best possible use of local village resources. This can help to drastically reduce the economic costs of farming.

Another crucial aspect is sustainability. As farmers' organizations are most closely related to their long-term welfare, they have to worry about the extent to which the natural fertility of land and soil has deteriorated, the extent to which water table is depleting, the extent to which natural pollinators are being destroyed, the extent to which GM crops threaten genetic pollution and other aspects of environmental ruin. The poisoning of farmers caused by highly toxic substances should be of immediate concern to them. As responsible citizens, they should be concerned about the production of safe and healthy food and the lowering of GHG emissions.

Keeping in view all this, farmers must demand that while government budget and subsidy for agriculture and related activities should go up greatly, this should directly reach small and medium farmers promoting and spreading ecologically protective agriculture. The rights of farmers to get a fair price for their produce should be respected.

At the same time, ecologically harmful and unsustainable systems should not be subsidized and should not be prolonged artificially with subsidies. The main principle is to move towards ecologically protective farming, without any single farmer being pushed towards losing livelihood, and extending government help to all farmers to earn a fair livelihood from ecologically protective farming.

While farmers in such an ecologically protective system have a priority claim for receiving adequate support from the government, they and their cooperatives/groups should be free to explore creative direct relationships with city-based consumers. One could allocate one urban colony to farmers from two or three villages where they have access to free, partially covered space for selling cereals, vegetables and milk without any restrictions on marketing or transport.

This acceptance of ecologically protective model will ensure a bright future for Indian farmers. Costs will decrease and the worldwide market for safe, healthy, organic, non-GMO food is certainly likely to increase. All health-conscious consumers are likely to be willing to pay a better price for healthy food. Sooner or later, it is likely that at the global level, better economic support will become available for food and other farm products produced in safe ways. Indian farming should try to move in the direction of providing healthy, safe, non-GM food and other farm products produced by small/medium farmers.

While asking farmers' organizations to support ecologically protective agriculture, I am aware that some sections use, or may use, ecology protection issues and organic food labels to indirectly serve certain narrow interests. We should be free from such interests, remain cautious and only think of genuine protection of agro-ecology. Let farmers prosper in sustainable ways and agro-ecology be protected carefully to make this possible.

In addition, farmers' movements should have a vision of widespread cottage/small-scale and village-level processing of cereals, millets, oilseeds, pulses, dairy products, fruits and vegetables, cotton and sugarcane. The way in which food processing is progressing provides few creative livelihoods for rural people. The bulk of the benefits go to big corporates or other city-based, capital-intensive enterprises. These often retard the emergence of small farmer-based enterprises.

14.4 We Need Different Paradigm

We hear about serious problems relating to farmers and farming and how to resolve them, generally in the context of three versions. One is of existing and upcoming big business interests who want to have an increasing role and ultimately dominate the farming sector. The second version is of the government which while supporting this corporatization tries also to dress this up in such a way that it may appear to be protecting the interests of farmers. The third version is of the mainstream farmers' movement whose main emphasis is on ensuring an adequate price for their produce.

Unfortunately, none of these versions is capable of resolving the crisis of farming and farming in a long-term, sustainable way. The long-term solutions have to be found outside the paradigm of these three dominant versions. Unfortunately, the media discussion is often confined to only these versions or a mix of them. On the basis of such discussions, we can at best get only temporary and patchy solutions, At worst, we will go from one crisis to another.

The big business interests have often talked in terms of GM crops, a new version being gene-edited crops. There is enough scientific evidence to show that this is nothing but a recipe for disaster. The government has often mentioned contract-based farming, with some safeguards, but past experience shows how this can be very harmful for ordinary small farmers.

The mainstream farmer movements have been pushing repeatedly for a higher price which is often stated by them to be 50 percent more than the broadly defined cost of cultivation. This has been discussed so often and emphasized so much as to create an impression that this provides an ultimate solution for the woes of farmers. The basic fallacy of this approach is neglected.

The problem with this perspective is that as soon as a price in certain excess of cost of cultivation is demanded, there is an implicit acceptance of rising costs. The most important task of decreasing costs of farming gets neglected. Since the advent of green revolution technology, the most important cause of increasing economic problems of farmers as well as their increasing debts relates to increasing costs of farming. So, the task of reducing costs is very important. A very important component of the increase in costs relates to the ever increasing price of industrial, cash-purchased inputs which harm farm ecology. So, we need to reduce these cash-purchased, costly, ecologically harmful inputs as much as possible making optimal use of village resources.

While this is eminently reasonable, industrial interests do not want this approach. Their earnings increase only when farmers purchase inputs from them. The media gets advertisement revenue mainly from industrial interests. Political leaders are often in collusion with industrial interests. There is increasing intrusion of big business in agricultural research and extension. Hence, what is most needed in the farming sector does not generally get support of the most powerful interests.

It is only farmers who can raise the most genuine demands. A lot of efforts are made to entice some of them or leaders towards raising their demands in such a way that the heavy dependence on industrial inputs is not reduced or disturbed. Hence the demand for keeping purchase price in certain excess of costs is raised. It can be 50 percent or 70 percent excess. This is not the real issue.

The real issue is that as soon as you present the main demand as a demand for a price in excess of costs, there is less incentive for deceasing costs. A leap in costs will only lead to a rise in the price the farmer will get. Having trapped the farmer in this narrow demand, politicians then compete for their vote by satisfying them within these narrow limits.

The danger is that the real objectives of justice, sustainability, protection of environment and creative durable livelihoods will be neglected. So, we have to move out of the current narrowly defined paradigm of farm debate. The solutions based on justice, sustainability, protection of environment, checking climate change and ensuring creative and durable livelihood to farmers as well as landless workers lie largely outside the current paradigm.

14.5 Non-Partisan View of Farmers' Movement

The farmers' movement in India has evoked strong feelings on both sides. It has been praised and criticism has been inflicted on it. It will be useful to attempt an unbiased appraisal.

The most persistent demand of this movement for the repeal of the three controversial laws is a justified demand. This has already been discussed. In addition, while these laws do not have any provision for taking over the land of farmers, as emphasized by the government, the overall impact of the tendencies promoted by the legislation will accelerate the trend of farmers becoming landless.

The farmers' movement deserves support for promoting the unity of people at several levels. It has promoted unity of farmers and unity of farmers with workers. It has promoted regional unity, particularly at the level of Punjab and Haryana which is welcome. This movement has promoted unity of various faiths and religions.

This movement deserves praise for its courage and determination which has been visible ever since it started. There has also been discipline and patience.

Nevertheless, despite its obvious strengths, the movement suffers from a number of limitations. The landless constitute the poorest segment of our rural population and their number is even higher than that of landowning farmers. What should be the agenda for them? What is the overall agenda for justice and equality for rural areas? This important issue is not been clear.

For sustainable livelihoods of farmers and for healthy ecologically protective farming along the lines of social agro-ecology is critical. But there has been no clear commitment yet from the farmers' movement that they want to move away from ecologically destructive farming. While asking for removing penal provisions for stubble burning, they should have said they are committed to reducing this. While justifiably backing subsidized irrigation, they should have said they will also work for promoting water conservation. On the whole, the movement needs to come out clearly in favour of ecologically protective farming.

14.6 Resisting Corporate Domination

Keeping in view the increasing concerns worldwide to check corporate control over farming and food systems, there is a need to be careful in various ways and means of resisting this.

Firstly, there is growing land grab. This can be more clearly seen in the purchase and long-term lease of land in Africa by companies, individuals or even governments of foreign countries. In just five countries during 2004-09 this amounted to 2.5 million hectares. But within various countries also corporate entities and rich individuals have been moving in quickly to grab at low rates the land of distressed small farmers. Governments in many countries have been handing over large tracts of land to corporate interests at concessional rates for plantations or crop cultivation. They have been making changes in their laws to facilitate this. Some Indian states too have been changing land ceiling and other laws.

There should be widespread national and global campaigns against all kinds of land grab and for cancelling the most unjust ones. Land in the hands of actual cultivators must be emphasized. Ownership of vast tracts of land by outsider entities should be opposed.

On the other hand, several big companies are not interested in accessing land directly. They feel an easier way of ensuring access to farm produce needed by them is through contract farming. The provisions of several contracts enable the companies to keep pushing their expensive inputs also on farmers so that they benefit from both ends. They get reliable supply of precisely the kind of crop needed by them (for example barley variety grown for making beer may be different from the variety needed for nutritious food) at a reasonable price. They retain the authority to reject a part of this crop on the grounds of quality. At the same time, they also earn from expensive seeds, inputs and technologies.

The reality of contract farming should be publicized among farmers and exploitative practices should be exposed. Where it is clear that farmers are suffering a lot, there should be a campaign for ending contract farming. The system of free cultivation by farmers should be protected.

Another form of gaining corporate domination is through excessive control of food processing. This should be resisted. In particular the domination of one or few big corporate entities should be resisted. More and more food processing should be taken up at village level by cooperatives and groups of farmers.

Another form of corporate control is through various international trade and financial organizations as well as trade treaties. The rules of the World Trade Organization should be changed in such a way that the interests of farmers are protected and unfair and unjust domination of the corporate sector is avoided. The trend to link farming and food related restrictions to trade, including intellectual property rights in trade, and imposing intellectual property rights in the context of even plants and life forms should be reversed. Trade should not be twisted and changed in such ways as to threaten the farming and food sovereignty of communities.

Domination of food trade and food stocks by corporate interests should be opposed. Ditto for manipulation of food stocks and hoarding. There should be strong laws to prevent this as well as monitor the national and international food stocks and prices.

There should be strong resistance to increasing concentration of seeds along with other important inputs in the hands of a few multinationals. There should be a ban on GM seeds and crops. At the same time, grassroot efforts to protect biodiversity and to save, protect, revive and share diversity of traditional seeds should be encouraged.

Corporate domination has been helped greatly by securing scientific support in unethical and unjust ways and by misusing infrastructure like research institutes, agricultural universities and gene banks. Research efforts should be decentralized. There should be a mutual cooperation of publicly supported scientists and experienced farmers to make available self-reliant, low cost, low external input, ecologically friendly and sustainable technologies. There should be strong efforts to expose and oppose unethical use of science to advance big business interests.

Corporate control in various forms seeks to break the self-reliance of farming communities. This process started in India in a big way about 55 years back with the green revolution and its extension to related activities. This led to rapidly increasing costs, loss of traditional seeds and wisdom as well as colossal ecological ruin. Efforts should be made by farming communities to regain lost self-reliance.

POSTSCRIPT

The decision of the government to repeal farm laws should be seen as one of the best and most eagerly awaited news to come from India in recent times. Of course, it would have been much better if this decision had been taken some months earlier, but better late than never.

We should first of all remember all the farmers who sacrificed their life in the course of the various strains and risks of the movement which continued through several extreme weather situations. This has been a great democratic struggle and it gives India great hope that it has ended on a note which is best described as a victory of democracy above everything else.

In this celebration of democracy of course the first tributes should be paid to the determination of farmers as well to their commitment to a peaceful and democratic struggle. At the same time credit should also be given to the government side for not standing on a false sense of prestige and opting for a very democratic solution. Some sporadic incidents had created a disturbing apprehension from time to time that at least some forces were trying to play certain kind of mischief to disrupt the movement. In the end the government did not permit such mischief beyond a point and on the whole opted for a democratic resolution of the long stand-off. For this the government deserves credit.

Some have argued that the government has done this mainly for electoral gains due to the forthcoming elections of Punjab and Uttar Pradesh. This may be a partial reason but this cannot be a complete explanation. When something really good is done by the government one should be generous and in this particular context the government has certainly displayed a commitmet to democracy for which it deserves praise.

The main demand being highlighted now relates to minimum support price. The government should be comitted to making available a fair price to farmers of course, but at the same time the government as well as the farmers' movement should also move in the direction of ecologically protective farming.

It should be realized by both sides that farming systems based on ecologically destructive practices which destroy basic resource base of soil and water, which kill pollinator birds and insects as well as soil builders like earthworms, which are energy intensive and directly as well as indirectly contribute to high greenhouse gas emissions are not sustainble and in addition these also lead inevitably to constant rise in costs. This constant rise of costs and destuction of soil, water, earthworms and pollinators is one of the most important causes of the crisis of farmers and farming.

So the way forward is for ecologically protective farming which can also help to reduce costs of farmers by increasing their self-reliance and by protecting their basic resource base of soil and water. We are in a fortunate positon today when the international funding for climate change mitigation and adaptation can additionally contribute much to such efforts. In addtion the government should also contribute more to promoting eco-friendly farming and this should become a mass movement. Already in a significant area of Andhra Pradesh and to a lesser extent in some other states like Sikkim and Himachal Pradesh, as well as in smaller pockets and projects in most states, we can see several successful examples of eco-friendly farming.

Last but not the least we should never forget the rural landless households who comprise the bottom half of our rural population. In their context also there is much room for their large-scale mobilization in tasks of ecological rehabilitation. As many as 67 economists have very recently written to the Prime Minister emphasizing the urgent need to increase MGNREGA funds (funds for rural employment guarantee). The Supreme Court has emphasized the need fpr community kitchens to reduce hunger. These are very good suggestions. In addition the neglected agenda of land reforms should be revived so that the landless can get at least some land.

We can only hope that the repeal of farm laws will prove to be only the first important step to be followed by other meaningful changes for farmers and farm workers and for the food and farming sector.

ACKNOWLEDGEMENTS

This book would not have been what it is without the support of Srishti Priya, Reshma Bharti and Madhu Dogra. Thank you for your help and encouragement.

My heartiest thanks to the editors of *Countercurrents.org*, *The Wire.in*, *Newsclick*, *The New Leam*, *The Statesman*, *The Mainstream*, *The Frontier* and other publications where some of these writings have been published before.

I would like to take this opportunity to also thank my publisher Renu Kaul Verma, my editor Narayan Swamy and the entire team at Vitasta Publishing for helping me through every stage of the book.

A huge thank you to my colleagues Kuldeep Kulshrestha and Ishwar Singh for their help.

And lastly, my gratitude to all the eminent personalities, authors as well as publishers who have been quoted in this book.

ABOUT THE AUTHORS

Bharat Dogra, 65, is a veteran journalist and author. He has written extensively on development, environment, human rights and social movements. He has reported from several remote areas, and received numerous journalism awards. As a whole, he has contributed around 9,500 articles and 400 books/booklets in English and Hindi including *Planet in Peril, Man Over Machine, When the Two Streams Met* and *Protecting Earth for Children*. His writings have consistently emphasized equality, justice, protection of livelihood, peace and non-violence, protection of environment and all forms of life. He has also been the honorary Chairperson of Jan Hith Trust and Convener of National Campaign for People's Right to Information. Currently, he is the Honorary Convener of Campaign to Save Earth with SED Demand.

Kumar Gautam, 42, is a teacher of Economics at The Lawrence School, Sanawar, Himachal Pradesh. He has been associated with the field of education, research and advocacy for over twenty years. While working with various national and international organisations, he has been passionately engaged in policy research and advocacy for favourable changes in the lives and livelihoods of farmers and artisans. He has been an articulate campaigner for a fair, equitable and sustainable agricultural trade policy while working for Oxfam's Global Campaigns, *Make Trade Fair* and *Economic Justice*. He has published several research articles, case studies and written many articles in journals and newspapers, both in English and Hindi.